sharing
prayer

sharing prayer

simple formats for small groups

mary sue taylor
of the mary and martha house

Nihil Obstat: Rev. Hilarion Kistner, O.F.M.
Rev. John J. Jennings

Imprimi Potest: Rev. Jeremy Harrington, O.F.M.
Provincial

Imprimatur: +James H. Garland, V.G.
Archdiocese of Cincinnati
August 26, 1987

The *nihil obstat* and *imprimatur* are a declaration that a book or pamphlet is considered to be free from doctrinal or moral error. It is not implied that those who have granted the *nihil obstat* and *imprimatur* agree with the contents, opinions or statements expressed.

Book and cover design by John Moores

ISBN 0-86716-086-1

To Mary Hughes
and Marilyn Elsen,
cofounders with me
of the Martha and Mary House.

And to all the women
and children
who find refuge
under its rafters.

contents

cycle 3

cycle 4

cycle 5

cycle 6

cycle 7

cycle 8

cycle 9

cycle 10

introduction

People interested in praying together are often stymied because they are not sure of how to go about it. Even those who have the know-how may lack the time needed for preparation. Groups which do form often have a few successful meetings but then stall. Many members of social action and charitable organizations who want to undergird their work with prayer don't quite know where to begin. And families who seek structures for prayer usually find nothing with staying power. This story varies, but it culminates in one question: How can we pray together?

This book offers a tested solution. It contains 90 prayer sessions based on five basic prayer formats. Each session is built around a biblical theme and accompanied by music, periods of silence and spontaneous prayer.

This book also offers a learning process. The formats are presented alternately in 10 cycles to keep your prayer sessions fresh and alive. Pray your way through the cycles and you will learn to plan your own sessions on the models given here.

Each cycle of sessions will let your group experience all of the formats. As you use this book, you will begin to adapt the formats to suit your own style: changing an opening or a closing, lengthening the periods of silence, developing your own meditation exercises, adding instruments—tambourines, castanets, drums, guitar—to the music. By the time you have prayed through this book, the formats will be familiar friends, and you will be able to structure your own prayer sessions.

the formats

The formats are: (1) Scripture Theme, (2) Psalm Theme, (3) Testament Threads, (4) Meditation Theme and (5) Collatio.

Scripture Themes pursue a theme through Scripture readings; commentaries and songs invite spontaneous prayer in response.

Psalm Themes weave poetic psalm passages around a common theme with music to match the mood.

Testament Threads are a collage of short verses which trace a thought through the Old and New Testaments. The verses are interwoven with periods of silence and song.

Meditation Themes include exercises designed to enable the pray-ers to experience God in their hearts rather than in their heads. Scripture readings and sacred songs prepare the ground for the exercises.

The goal of meditation, or contemplation, is a mystical experience of God. Such experiences are not reserved to saints and hermits; you may have them too, if the Lord chooses to gift you in this way. But to receive a gift, you must hold out your hands. The purpose of these prayer sessions is to still your mind and body so that you can develop your openness to God and God's gifts. The exercises will open your hands and your hearts to receive whatever experience the Lord is trying to give you. If, at any time during a meditation exercise, you feel a pull to let go of the exercise and just dwell in the presence of the Lord, *do so*. That is precisely what should happen!

Collatio is a Latin word (pronounced co-*lah*-tsee-o) for a shared meal to which everyone contributes and in which everyone shares—a Roman potluck supper. Here the word describes a structured, prayerful sharing of insights after listening to a Scripture reading. Questions to spark sharing are provided for use as needed. The sharing is intended to be a reflection of personal experience, not a sermon for others. Comments should be short—a few sentences; the sharing should *not* turn into a discussion. Be at ease with the silent gaps between comments; be enriched by the sharing which, as spiritual writer Armand Nigro puts it, "can transform the spiritual lives of families and groups."

setting the scene for prayer

Comfortable chairs and floor pillows provide a relaxed and prayerful setting. Since concentration improves when pray-ers are not visually distracted, darkening the room is helpful. You might also want to unplug the phone. You will usually need your Bible, a candle and a small reading lamp or a flashlight.

Choose a person to lead each prayer session. The leader assigns the readings in advance, opens the session and announces the theme, paces the session, coordinates the music, signals readers and closes the prayer. This role, as well as the role of reader, can be rotated among the group members.

Silence is an important element in these prayer sessions. Two kinds of silence are indicated: A *Pause*, normally 30 to 60 seconds (longer if you wish), follows the readings and allows time for the listeners to absorb what they have heard. The word *Silence* after a reading or a song signals a more protracted stillness—five to 20 minutes—in which to be sensitive to the presence of God and the movement of the Spirit. The more often you come together, the more comfortable your group will be with shared silence. This silent time will be like water to the Word which falls as seed on the ground of your being.

Music suggested in these prayer sessions is all taken from these seven albums or tapes:

> *The God of Life* (John Michael Talbot)
> *Cry Hosanna* (Fisherfolk)
> *Calm Is the Night* (the Monks of Weston Priory)
> *I Will Not Forget You* (Carey Landry)
> *No Longer Strangers* (John Michael Talbot)
> *A Dwelling Place* (the St. Louis Jesuits)
> *Wood Hath Hope* (John Foley)

These recordings were selected because, as a group, they offer a good variety of songs for both inspiration and celebration. You may, of course, substitute your own choice.

---

a group to pray with

These prayer sessions were developed by an unusual group: the residents of the Mary and Martha House in Ruskin, Florida. A refuge for women, alone or with children, who are without resources and need a fresh start in life, the Mary and Martha House welcomes guests for several weeks while they try to become self-sufficient. Over 450 women and children have passed through its doors since its opening in 1982. Supported by donations from individuals and various Church and civic groups, the Mary and Martha House offers its services at no charge.

Most of its guests find work within the first week or two of their stay and remain long enough to save for a rent deposit on their own place. Staff and volunteers serve as advocates for these women, counseling them in such down-to-earth matters as budgeting, personal hygiene and job-hunting.

And at least one evening a week, everyone who so chooses gathers to pray together. It is that prayer this book seeks to share.

If you have no ready-made group, ask a friend, a family member or a neighbor to pray with you. If no one seems to share your interest in prayer, begin alone. Even at the Mary and Martha House, sometimes the only participants besides the resident volunteer are Butch and Bubbles, the community's dogs. Alone or with others, the routine is the same. Set a time and place for prayer each week—and stick with it. Set the scene as described above, adding whatever is meaningful to you.

Then simply follow the prayer formats in this book and allow them to lead you through your prayer sessions. Mention to a few like-minded individuals when and where you pray and keep open the invitation to join you.

A family is a ready-made group for praying together, and this book can be adapted for family prayer. Even small children love to gather for prayer. They absorb more through their hearts than through their heads, sensing the warmth, love and openness that envelops the prayer sessions. Hand-holding, hugging, stroking and simple spontaneous prayer are especially stimulating to little ones. Don't worry if the children fall asleep during the prayer—prayer is a wonderful send-off to the land of dreams.

To adapt these prayer formats to children, have a children's Bible on hand. After the Scripture reading, read the same passage a second time from the children's Bible. (An older child can do this reading.) The one prayer format that probably will not be appropriate for most youngsters is the Meditation Theme because of its long periods of silence. Save these exercises for times when young children are not present.

a final word

Whether you pray in solitude or in community, you bring the power of divine intervention and healing to your neighborhood and to all other groups with which you interact. As others become aware of your "public prayer time," they will bring their petitions to you. And the rest is up to the Holy Spirit.

cycle 1

SCRIPTURE THEME:

'Blessed Are the Meek'

Opening
Let us begin our prayer by closing our eyes and calming our thoughts so that we become aware of the presence of God.

> *Pause*

Song
"The Servant Song" from *Cry Hosanna*, by Fisherfolk

First Reading
Matthew 5:5, RSV ("Blessed are the meek.")

Second Reading
Psalm 37 ("The meek shall possess the land.")

> *Pause*

Commentary
From a sermon by Rev. Larry Henderson:

> *Meek* means strength under control. A horse which was once wild but which has become obedient to the bit and the bridle is considered meek. The horse, once tamed, does not lose any of its strength, agility or speed. In fact, when tamed or meek, it can pull heavier loads and run faster because it is under control.
>
> Christians are people tamed by God. To be tamed by God's love changes the way one thinks and acts; it brings responsibilities, fidelity to the tamer and a concern for the untamed.
>
> Jesus is the person who shows us what it means to be meek. When the Roman soldiers hung Christ on

the cross, he was still under enough control to pray, "Forgive them, Father, for they know not what they do."

Song
"Behold the Wood" from *A Dwelling Place*, by the St. Louis Jesuits

Silence

Spontaneous Prayer

Closing
Join hands and say the Our Father.

PSALM THEME:

Praise God

Opening
Let us begin our prayer by praising God in song.

Song
"Glory and Praise to Our God" from *A Dwelling Place*, by the St. Louis Jesuits

Readings
Psalm 150 ("Let everything praise the Lord!")

Silence

Psalm 148 (Praise the Lord in all creation.)

Silence

Psalm 92:1-4 (Praise for the Lord's goodness)

Silence

Song
"In Praise of His Name" from *A Dwelling Place*, by the St. Louis Jesuits

Silence

Spontaneous Prayer

Closing
"In Praise of God," by Edna Fraser.*

The Lord works in wondrous ways. I believe he made me blind so that I might see.

He left me enough sight so I might behold his world in muted shades of green, the sun sparkling upon the calm waters, the blue of the sky, his awesome power as he unleashes it in his thunderstorms....

He is so grand, words cannot really explain him.

He has given in such abundance my cup truly runs over. He has given me true friends with welcoming smiles, the warmth of hands outstretched to help, the companionship of conversation, the special benefit of prayer in the evening.

He has at times laid ever so gently upon me his cross. I have faltered, but...he has understood.

He has given me so much, how can I possibly tell it all? The happy chatter of children at play, the welcoming wagging of puppies' tails.

He has helped me see the inner beauty in all people.

For the help he is giving me in having my sight restored, thank you, Lord.

But I thank him most for the chance to grow as a person. May I become strong enough to help at least one other person who is in need. Amen.

SCRIPTURE THEME:

Self-Knowledge

Opening
Lord, we open our prayer asking for the grace to turn our eyes inward upon ourselves. This is the revolution that will change the heart of humanity.

---

* Edna was a 52-year-old blind lady who stayed at the Mary and Martha House for six months while she was having cataract surgery. On the way to a doctor's appointment, she was killed in an automobile accident.

Song
"Holy God of Truth" from *The God of Life*, by John Michael Talbot

First Reading
Matthew 7:3-5 (The speck in your brother's eye)

Pause

Second Reading
From the writings of Carl Jung in *The Portable Jung*:

> No matter how much the parents and grandparents may have sinned against the child, the person who is really adult will accept these sins as his own condition which has to be reckoned with. Only a fool is interested in other people's guilt since he cannot alter it. The wise man learns only from his own guilt. He will ask himself: Who am I that this should happen to me? To find the answer to this fateful question, he will look into his own heart.

Silence

Third Reading
Luke 8:16-18 (The hidden will be known.)

Pause

Fourth Reading
Psalm 139:1-18 (The all-knowing God)

Song
"The Spirit Within Us" from *Calm Is the Night*, by the Monks of Weston Priory

Silence

Spontaneous Prayer

Closing
We end our prayer asking for the courage to keep looking inward.

The Jesus Prayer

Opening
We begin our prayer in the name of Jesus.

Song
"Dwelling Place" from *A Dwelling Place*, by the St. Louis Jesuits

Readings
1 Thessalonians 5:15-18 ("Never cease praying.")

> *Pause*

Ephesians 6:18 ("Pray constantly.")

> *Pause*

1 Timothy 2:8 (In every place people should pray.)

> *Pause*

Meditation Exercise
The Jesus prayer is a short, simple prayer that is repeated over and over in rhythm with the breath. This prayer fulfills Paul's injunction to pray constantly. Once this prayer has been practiced and integrated with your breathing, it will pray itself in your heart.

The prayer is simply this: "Lord Jesus Christ, have mercy on me."

Say "Lord Jesus Christ" as you breathe in, and imagine you are breathing in divine love and power. You really are, after all, since the Word has life. Then, when you breathe out, say "Have mercy on me." Imagine that all of your fears and shortcomings leave when you breathe out. They will begin to leave you as you ceaselessly breathe Jesus Christ into your heart. If you are uncomfortable with the word *mercy* (as many Westerners are), keep in mind that you are not asking for pity but acknowledging the authority of God and Jesus in your life.

Close your eyes now and begin to repeat the Jesus prayer over and over. As you breathe in, say "Lord Jesus Christ." As you breathe out, say "Have mercy on me."

> Lord Jesus Christ, have mercy on me.
> Lord Jesus Christ, have mercy on me.

Lord Jesus Christ, have mercy on me.

Silence

Song

"Brother Jesus" from *I Will Not Forget You*, by Carey Landry

Pause

Spontaneous Prayer

Closing

We close our prayer in gratitude, knowing that it is in you, Lord, that we live and move and have our being.

SCRIPTURE THEME:

Letting Go

Opening

Let us take a minute to let go of our cares and become aware of God's presence around us.

Song

"Lose Yourself in Me" from *I Will Not Forget You*, by Carey Landry

Reading

Matthew 6:25-34 (Do not worry.)

Pause

Commentary

If you are waiting to be happy until you meet the perfect lover, or get the perfect job, or find the perfect place to live, you are in hell, the hell of not being satisfied with what the moment brings. Your restlessness for something else—something that is not happening to you right now—that is what causes unhappiness.

For a few minutes now, let us try to let go of hell. Let us let go of the things that are bothering us, the things that are keeping us from experiencing the moment right now. Are we worrying about some of our relationships? Did we hurt someone? Did someone hurt us? Let go of that hurt and give it to God.

Pause

Pretend you are holding three balloons. In your imagination, write the name of a worry or care on each balloon. Let go of each balloon slowly—one at a time. Watch each balloon float away. Read the name on the balloon as it flies away.

Silence

Song
"For We Are Free" and the "Gospel Reading" which immediately follows it from *Calm Is the Night*, by the Monks of Weston Priory

Silence

Spontaneous Prayer

Closing
Our prayer is ended. Let us go forth in peace.

Water of Life

Opening
Let all who are thirsty for God come now and drink the waters of eternal life.

Song
"Come to the Water" from *Wood Hath Hope*, by John Foley, S. J.

Readings
Psalm 42:2:
As the hind longs for the running waters,
    so my soul longs for you, O God.

Pause

Isaiah 55:1a:
All you who are thirsty,
    come to the water!

Pause

Isaiah 55:1b:
You who have no money,

come, receive grain and eat;
Come, without paying and without cost,
   drink wine and milk!

Pause

Isaiah 55:2a:
Why spend your money for what is not bread;
   your wages for what fails to satisfy?

Pause

Isaiah 55:6:
Seek the LORD while he may be found,
   call him while he is near.

Pause

Isaiah 55:8:
For my thoughts are not your thoughts,
   nor are your ways my ways.

Pause

John 4:14:
"...the water I give
shall become a fountain within him,
leaping up to provide eternal life."

Pause

John 7:37-38:
"If anyone thirsts, let him come to me;
let him drink who believes in me.
Scripture has it:
'From within him rivers of living water shall flow.'"

Song
"Fill My Cup Lord" from *Cry Hosanna*, by Fisherfolk

Silence

Spontaneous Prayer

Closing
Father, we close our prayer, giving thanks to you for the waters
that refresh our soul.

Healing

Opening
Let us begin our prayer in the name of God our Father.

Pause

The power of prayer is the greatest force on earth—especially when it is combined with actions which reflect the will of God. Our intercession is important because the Lord needs us as his vessels of healing. If we do not allow ourselves to be vessels of grace, God's graces cannot flow freely. It is a mystery, but it seems to be God's way of sharing power with us.

Pause

Songs
"Litany," "Healing Prayer" and "The Lord's Prayer" from *Calm Is the Night*, by the Monks of Weston Priory

Silence

First Reading
Ephesians 3:14-21 (Asking God's power)

Pause

Second Reading
John 14:12-14 (Jesus' power in his disciples)

Pause

Third Reading
Matthew 18:19-20 (Gathered in Jesus' name)

Song
"Healer of My Soul" from *The God of Life*, by John Michael Talbot

Pause

Instructions for Laying On of Hands
The person to be prayed over should sit in the center of the group. The others encircle the person and place a hand on her or him. It is up to each person to choose the way he or she wants to pray—silently or aloud, spontaneously or using this prayer:

Lord, may your spirit descend upon
our hands to provide healing graces
for _____.
Glory be to the Father, the Son and
the Holy Spirit. Amen.

Laying On of Hands

Closing
Holding the same position, close by saying the Lord's Prayer
together.

MEDITATION THEME:

The Sounds of Creation

Opening
Let us begin our prayer with hearts grateful for the sounds of
creation.

Song
"Monastery Bells" and "Spirit Within Us" from *Calm Is the Night*,
by the Monks of Weston Priory

Reading
Psalm 104:5-24 (The majesty of creation)

Silence

Meditation Exercise
Sounds can give us a great appreciation of nature and its Creator.
Even sounds which are considered annoying or disturbing may be
appreciated if we accept rather than resist them.

Close your eyes now and listen to the sounds from the majesty
of God's creation: the wind in the trees, the crickets, the whir of
traffic and children laughing. Listen also, with a welcoming ear,
to those noises which usually irritate you: barking dogs or sirens.
Let these noises flow through you. Lose yourself to this world of
sound.

Silence

Imagine the world if there were no sounds. Imagine your world if you lost your sense of hearing. Let your heart fill with gratefulness to God for the gift of sound.

> *Silence*

Song
"Only in God" from *A Dwelling Place*, by the St. Louis Jesuits

Closing
We end our prayer in thanksgiving for the gift of sound. Amen.

COLLATIO:

'Take Up Your Cross'

Song
"Few Be the Lovers" from *No Longer Strangers*, by John Michael Talbot

Opening
The theme of our prayer is taking up the cross. You will each have the opportunity to share aloud what the Scripture reading means to you, so please listen attentively and allow the Scripture to speak to you personally.

> *Pause*

Lord, free us from anxiety and fear so that we may open our ears and our hearts to your Word.

> *Pause*

First Reading
Matthew 16:24-28 ("Take up your cross.")

> *Pause*

Instructions
Each person may now share aloud what the Scripture meant to him or her. The sharing is intended to be a reflection of personal experience, not a sermon for others. Keep comments short—a few sentences. This sharing should not turn into discussion. Be at ease with the silent gaps between comments.

If needed, the following questions may spark more sharing:

1) Why did Jesus say, "Take up your cross," rather than "Accept your cross"?

2) How would you change your life if you were going to live these words?

Sharing

The same passage will be read aloud again. As you listen to it this time, reflect on the comments each person shared with the group.

Second Reading
Matthew 16:24-28

Instructions
There will be a period of silence and then spontaneous prayer. The prayers spoken aloud should relate to the reading and its effect on you. For instance, "Father, give me strength to take up my cross," or "Jesus, help me live these words in my everyday life."

Silence

Spontaneous Prayer

Closing Song
"Behold the Wood" from *A Dwelling Place*, by the St. Louis Jesuits

cycle 2

SCRIPTURE THEME:

Bread of Life

Opening
We shall not live by bread alone, but by every word that proceeds from the mouth of God. (cf. Matthew 4:4)

Pause

Song
"Gift of Finest Wheat" from *Cry Hosanna*, by Fisherfolk

First Reading
John 6:25-27 ("Do not labor for food which perishes.")

Pause

Second Reading
John 6:32-40 (The Bread of Life)

Pause

Third Reading
John 6:48-58 (Anyone who eats of the heavenly bread will have eternal life.)

Song
"One Bread, One Body" from *Wood Hath Hope*, by John Foley, S.J.

Silence

Suggestion
For spontaneous prayer join hands and say the Our Father; then lift your prayer offerings.

Spontaneous Prayer

Closing

Lord, we close our prayer by sharing bread and wine together. We thank you for this our daily bread and pray that we use your gifts to nourish one another.

Suggestion

If possible, use a loaf of homemade bread (unsliced) and red wine. Make the bread (already on a breadboard with a knife), wine and wine glasses the focal points for the prayer gathering—maybe by placing them on the same table as the candle. If no one has time to bake bread, you can usually buy whole loaves at the supermarket delicatessen. Slice the bread right before serving.

This close is a celebration of Christian fellowship and good conversation should flow freely. Don't think you have to be guarded or formal during this joyful sharing.

PSALM THEME:

Dwelling Place

Opening

As we open our prayer we open our hearts to provide a permanent dwelling place for love.

Pause

Song

"Dwelling Place" from *A Dwelling Place,* by the St. Louis Jesuits

First Reading

Psalm 84 (God's dwelling place)

Silence

Psalm 15 (God's guest)

Silence

Psalm 24 (The Lord's entry)

Silence

Psalm 43 ("Bring me to your dwelling place.")

> *Silence*

Song

"Only in God" from *A Dwelling Place,* by the St. Louis Jesuits

> *Silence*

> *Spontaneous Prayer*

Closing

Our prayer together is ended. As we go about our daily affairs, let us continue to dwell in the house of the Lord.

SCRIPTURE THEME:

Forgiveness

Opening

Let us begin our prayer with a period of reflection on the day, asking forgiveness of those we have offended and forgiving those who have offended us.

Song

"Trust In the Lord" from *A Dwelling Place,* by the St. Louis Jesuits

First Reading

Matthew 5:21-26 ("First be reconciled.")

> *Pause*

Second Reading

Matthew 18:21-35 (The merciless official)

> *Pause*

Third Reading

Luke 17:1-4 (We must forgive one another.)

Suggestion

During the silent time, pray the Lord's Prayer to yourself. As you say the prayer, notice that most of it is about God and his Kingdom. The only requirement of us is that we forgive one another. And the more easily we can forgive our sister or brother, the more easily we can forgive ourselves. However, to look at our sin, look at our guilt and acknowledge it before God is very difficult for most of us. It is easier to deny our wrongdoing. This denial not only leads to self-righteousness and puffed-up pride but to an unforgiving attitude toward others. Sin is destructive behavior and if we refuse to own up to our destructive ways, we will never outgrow them. Forgiveness, on the other hand, is constructive because it heals our wounds and allows us to build bridges to one another. Forgiveness is at the heart of the gospel message because it unlocks the "narrow door" to love of self and others.

Pause

Song

"Healer of My Soul" from *The God of Life*, by John Michael Talbot

Silence

Spontaneous Prayer

Closing

We close our prayer with the words of the psalmist:

My sacrifice, O God, is a contrite spirit;
> a heart contrite and humbled, O God, you will not
> > spurn. (Psalm 51:19)
Amen.

'Be Still and Know That I Am God'

Opening

Let us begin our prayer by taking a minute or two to still our hearts so that we can become more aware of God's presence within us.

Silence

Song

"Calm Is the Night" from *Calm Is the Night*, by the Monks of Weston Priory

Readings

Better is a handful of quietness than two hands full of toil and a striving after wind. (Ecclesiastes 4:6, RSV)

Pause

And the effect of righteousness will be peace,
and the result of righteousness, quietness and trust forever.
(Isaiah 32:17, RSV)

Pause

"Be still, and know that I am God.
  I am exalted among the nations,
  I am exalted in the earth!"
The Lord of hosts is with us;
  the God of Jacob is our refuge. (Psalm 46 [45]:10-11, RSV)

Pause

Meditation Exercise
God's Kingdom is here right now. To become more aware of the Lord's presence among us, however, we must be still. First we must still ourselves physically; then we must still ourselves mentally.

Pause

Sit in a comfortable position with your back straight. Your eyes may be opened or closed, whichever you prefer. Try not to move—in a sense, "freeze" your position. You will be amazed at the effect that stilling your bodily motions has on your mind. As you bring your body under control, your mind will follow.

Enter now into the stillness, remembering the psalmist's words: "Be still and know that I am God."

Instructions
The first time the group does this exercise, cut the silence off after five to seven minutes. After that, keep extending it until you reach 20 minutes.

Silence

Song
"God" from *The God of Life*, by John Michael Talbot

Silence

Spontaneous Prayer

Closing
Join hands and say the Lord's Prayer.

Evil Tongues

Opening
"In the beginning was the Word;
  and the Word was in God's presence,
  and the Word was God." (John 1:1)

  Pause

Song
"The Word Who Is Life" from *I Will Not Forget You,* by Carey Landry

First Reading
Psalm 12 (Deceitful tongues)

  Pause

Second Reading
James 3:1-12 (Uncontrolled language)

  Pause

Third Reading
From *The Imitation of Christ,* by Thomas à Kempis:

> Fly the hubbub of men as much as you can; for concern
> with worldy affairs is a great hindrance, although they
> be entered into with a good intention. For we are soon
> tainted by vanity and held captive. Often I have wished
> that I had been silent after having been in the company
> of men.
>
> But why are we so willing to talk and discourse
> with one another, even though we seldom return to
> silence without hurt of conscience?
>
> The reason why we are so willing to talk is because
> by discoursing together we seek consolation from one
> another and we wish to ease our heart, wearied by
> various thoughts. And we are fond of speaking and

thinking of such things that we very much love and desire, or of which we imagine allows us to argue.

But alas, it is often in vain, and to no purpose; for this outward consolation is no small hindrance to inward and divine consolation.

Therefore, we must watch and pray, that our time pass not idly away. If it be lawful and expedient to speak, speak only those things which may edify.

Bad habits and a negligence of our spiritual development are the main causes of our keeping so little guard on our tongue. But devout conferences on spiritual things help very much in spiritual progress, especially where persons of the same mind and spirit are associated together in God.

Silence

Fourth Reading
Sirach 5:11-14 ("Be steady in your convictions, sincere in your speech.")

Pause

Song
"Holy God of Truth" from *The God of Life,* by John Michael Talbot

Silence

Spontaneous Prayer

Closing
We close our prayer, heavenly Father, with the resolve to be sincere in speech.

TESTAMENT THREADS:

'Love Your Neighbor as Yourself'

Opening
Lord of the universe, help us to see your beauty shining through all of creation, particularly those whose religious beliefs differ from ours. Let us rejoice in our similarities and celebrate our unity.

Song

"Neighbors" from *Cry Hosanna*, by Fisherfolk

Instructions

While reading the following phrases, play music softly in the background. A suggested song for this purpose is "Servants" from *Cry Hosanna*, by Fisherfolk.

Readings

The Golden Rule is a part of every major religion. Here is the way different religions phrase the rule:

Christianity: "You shall love your neighbor as yourself " (Matthew 22:39b).

> *Pause*

Buddhism: One would seek for others the happiness one desires for one's self. Hurt no others in ways that you yourself would find hurtful.

> *Pause*

Confucianism: Do not unto others what you would not have them do to you.

> *Pause*

Parsiism: Do as you would be done by.

> *Pause*

Hinduism: The true rule is to do by the things of others as you do by your own.

> *Pause*

Brahmanism: This is the sum of duty: Do not unto others which would cause you pain if done to you.

> *Pause*

Taoism: Regard your neighbor's gain as your own gain, and your neighbor's loss as your own loss.

> *Pause*

Zoroastrianism: That nature alone is good which refrains from doing unto another whatsoever is not good for itself.

Pause

Judaism: What is hateful to you do not do to your fellow man.

Pause

Islam: No one of you is a believer until he desires for his brother that which he desires for himself.

Pause

Song
Allow the background song to play out; then play "One Bread, One Body" from *Wood Hath Hope*, by John Foley, S. J.

Silence

Spontaneous Prayer

Closing
Stand in a circle, join hands and pray in silence for one minute.

The Shepherd

Opening
"I am the good shepherd.
  I know my sheep
  and my sheep know me." (John 10:14)

Song
"Like a Shepherd" from *A Dwelling Place*, by the St. Louis Jesuits

First Reading
John 10:1-18 (The Good Shepherd)

Pause

Second Reading
Psalm 23 ("The Lord is my shepherd.")

Pause

Third Reading
Matthew 18:10-14 (The lost sheep)

Pause

Suggestion

During the silent time, you might want to reflect on the infinity of divine love. Each one of us is a lost sheep when we stray from God because of destructive behavior, rebellion or lack of faith. Not only does God welcome us back after we turn from him, he goes out to find us and volunteers to carry us back to his graces. Imagine the immensity of such love. Lose yourself in gratefulness.

Song

"Come to the Water" from *Wood Hath Hope,* by John Foley, S. J.

Silence

Spontaneous Prayer

Closing

We close our prayer with a quote from Isaiah:

> Like a shepherd he feeds his flock;
>   in his arms he gathers the lambs,
> Carrying them in his bosom,
>   and leading the ewes with care. (Isaiah 40:11)

MEDITATION THEME:

A Place of Prayer

Opening

Let us begin our prayer, eager to find that dwelling place of the Lord within us.

Song

"Dwelling Place" from *A Dwelling Place,* by the St. Louis Jesuits

Reading

Psalm 84 (God's dwelling place)

Pause

Meditation Exercise

When you pick a place to pray, pick a spot that helps you feel closer to God—a spot that is relaxing and peaceful. Since nature brings people closer to God, close your eyes now and imagine a landscape setting that is likely to inspire you. Imagine a seashore with the waves lapping up on the beach, a snowy mountain peak, a garden full of beautiful flowers or a woods where the sunlight is filtering down through the trees. Fix the place as clearly as possible and hold this picture in your mind. If you are distracted, just go right back to the picture. After you have fixed the image in your mind a while, raise your heart to the Lord and say something to him.

> *Silence*

Song

"A Place to Go" from *Calm Is the Night*, by the Monks of Weston Priory.

> *Pause*

> *Spontaneous Prayer*

Closing

Father, we close our prayer, thanking you for your presence among us and for listening to the prayers of our hearts.

COLLATIO:

The Good Samaritan

Song

"Neighbors" from *Cry Hosanna*, by Fisherfolk

Opening

The theme of our prayer is the Good Samaritan. You will each have the opportunity to share aloud what the Scripture reading meant to you, so please listen attentively and allow the Scripture to speak to you personally.

> *Pause*

Speak to us Lord. Help us listen to your Word and to enjoy being silent in each other's presence.

Pause

First Reading
Luke 10:25-37 (The Good Samaritan)

Silence

Instructions
Each person may now share aloud what the Scripture meant to him or her. The sharing is intended to be a reflection of personal experience, not a sermon for others. Keep comments short—just a few sentences. The sharing should not turn into discussion. Be at ease with the silent gaps between comments.

Sharing

The same passage will be read aloud again. As you listen to it this time, reflect on the comments each person shared with the group.

Second Reading
Luke 10:25-37

Instructions
There will be a period of silence and then spontaneous prayer. The prayers spoken aloud should relate to the reading and its effect on you. For example, "Give me the grace to be compassionate," or, "Lord of Creation, help me to see you in all creatures."

Silence

Spontaneous Prayer

Closing Song
"One Bread, One Body" from *Wood Hath Hope*, by John Foley, S.J.

Sharing Aids
If needed, the following questions might spark more sharing and can be used by the leader during the first sharing session.
1. The traveler in the Good Samaritan story probably was careless and didn't plan ahead since most people in that day traveled in caravans for security. The helper, however, makes no judgment but, instead, reaches out in charity and brotherly love.

2. The Samaritan did as much for the traveler as he could, rather than just patching him up so he could "get by." How does this compare with our modern-day philosophy of giving?

cycle 3

Discernment

Opening

We begin our prayer for discernment by lifting our souls to you, Yahweh.

Song

"I Lift Up My Soul" from *A Dwelling Place,* by the St. Louis Jesuits.

First Reading

Psalm 25 (Prayer for guidance and help)

Pause

Second Reading

1 John 2:15-17 (The one who does God's will lives forever.)

Pause

Commentary

"The world with its seductions is passing away" (1 John 2:17). The only thing in our lives that is not temporary is our prayer relationship with God—which is found in silence. The more we get to know God in the silence of our hearts, the easier it is for us to discern God's will for us. The better listeners we become, the better we understand what will please God. For discernment to happen, silence must be an important part of our lives.

Silence

Song

"Holy God of Truth" from *The God of Life,* by John Michael Talbot

Pause

Closing
Join hands for a minute of silent prayer.

PSALM THEME:

Refuge

Opening
Let us begin our prayer with a few minutes of silence, putting away the cares of the day and seeking refuge in the Lord.

Silence

First Reading
Psalm 91 (God's protection)

Pause

Song
"Blest Be the Lord" from *A Dwelling Place*, by the St. Louis Jesuits

Second Reading
Psalm 31:1-9 (Taking refuge in God)

Silence

Third Reading
Psalm 31:20-25 (The Lord's care)

Pause

Song
"Calm Is the Night" from *Calm Is the Night*, by the Monks of Weston Priory

Silence

Closing
We close our prayer, Lord, thanking you for being our rock and our refuge. Amen.

'Blessed Are the Peacemakers'

Opening
Let us begin our prayer in the spirit of peace.

Song
"Peace Is Flowing Like a River" from *I Will Not Forget You*, by Carey Landry

First Reading
John 14:25-31 (Christ's gift of peace)

> *Silence*

Second Reading
Matthew 5:9 (The peacemakers)

> *Pause*

Third Reading
From a legend of the early Christian hermits:

> Three friends were eager to live out the Beatitude, "Blessed are the peacemakers." One chose to live out the Beatitude by making peace between people who were fighting with each other. The second chose to visit the sick. The third went off to live in the desert.
>
> The first one toiled away trying to solve the quarrels of others, but could not. In discouragement, he decided to go visit his friend who was tending the sick. When he found him he discovered that he too was floundering in his efforts to be a peacemaker.
>
> They agreed to go and visit the hermit, who was living in the desert. When they got there, they found that their friend's very presence emanated peace. "What is your secret?" they asked. The hermit was silent for a time. Then he poured some water into a bowl and said to them, "Look at the water." It was all turbulent. A little later he told them to look at it again and see how the water had settled down. When they looked at it they saw their own faces as in a mirror. Then he said to them, "In the same way one who is living in the midst of people does not see his own sins because of all the

disturbance. But if he becomes tranquil, then he can see his own shortcomings."

The hermit paused and then continued, "If you would have peace you must first begin with yourself. To become a peacemaker, you must acknowledge your own shortcomings and begin to make peace between the warring elements within yourself."

Song
"Peace to You" from *Calm Is the Night*, by the Monks of Weston Priory

Silence

Suggestion
Stand in a circle, join hands and say the Lord's Prayer together. Remain with hands joined for spontaneous prayer.

Spontaneous Prayer

Closing
Let us close our prayer by offering one another a gesture of peace—a handshake, a hug or a kiss.

MEDITATION THEME:

Reverence for All Creation

Preparation
Ask each participant to bring to the session some small, frequently used object.

Opening
We open our prayer, divine Father, reminding ourselves that we are your children. Help us to develop that childlike quality of finding wonder and amazement in all things.

Song
"O Clap Your Hands" from *Cry Hosanna*, by Fisherfolk

Suggestion
(Create a festival atmosphere by handclapping or provide spoons and pans to bang along with the music.)

Readings

Mark 10:13-15 (The children)

Pause

Matthew 11:25-26 (Revealed to babes)

Pause

Meditation Exercise

From *Sadhana*, by Anthony de Mello, S. J.:

This exercise is to help you develop an attitude of reverence and respect for all of creation, for all the objects that surround you. To do this you will have to temporarily put aside your adult prejudices and become like a little child that will talk to its doll. If you become a little child, at least temporarily, you might discover a kingdom of heaven—and learn secrets that God ordinarily hides from the wise and prudent.

Choose some object that you use frequently: a pen, a cup, a piece of jewelry. It should be an object that you can easily hold in your hands...an object that you have had a while and has meaning to you.

Let the object rest on the palms of your outstretched hands. Now close your eyes and get the feel of it on your palms. Become as fully aware of it as possible. First become aware of its weight—then of the sensation it produces on your palms.

Now explore it with your fingers or with both your hands. It is important that you do this gently and reverently: explore its roughness or smoothness, its hardness or softness, its warmth or coldness. Now touch it to other parts of your body and see if it feels different. Touch it to your lips, your cheeks, your forehead, the back of your hand.

Turn on a light

You have become acquainted with your object through your sense of touch. Now become acquainted with it, become aware of it, through your sense of sight. Open your eyes and look at it from different angles. See every possible detail in it: its colors, its form, its various parts.

Turn the light back off

Smell it, taste it, if possible, hear it by placing it close to your ear. Now gently place the object in front of you or on your lap and speak to it. Begin by asking it questions about itself. How did it come into your life? Did you buy it or did someone give it to you? Why do you have it? Listen while it unfolds to you the secret of its being and of its destiny. Listen while it explains to you what existence means to it.

Pause

Your object has some hidden wisdom to reveal to you about yourself. Ask for this and listen to what it has to say. There is something that you can give this object. What is it? What does it want from you?

Silence

Now place yourself and this object in the presence of Jesus Christ, the Word of God, in whom and for whom everything was made. Listen to what he has to say to you and to the object. What do the two of you say in response?

Silence

Now look at your object once more. Has your attitude toward it changed? Is there any change in your attitude toward the other objects around you?

Pause

Song
"Fill My Cup, Lord" from *Cry Hosanna,* by Fisherfolk

Pause

Spontaneous Prayer

Closing
We close our prayer in gratefulness for all of creation.

SCRIPTURE THEME:

Personal Prayer

Opening
"Here I stand, knocking at the door. If anyone hears me calling

and opens the door, I will enter his house and have supper with him, and he with me" (Revelation 3:20).

Pause

Song
"Holy God of Truth" from *The God of Life,* by John Michael Talbot

First Reading
Matthew 6:5-6 (How to pray)

Pause

Second Reading
In *A Self-Emptied Heart,* Henri Nouwen encourages us through the difficulties of personal prayer:

> For most of us, it is very hard to spend a useless hour with God. It is hard precisely because facing God alone we also face our own inner chaos. We come in direct confrontation with our restlessness, anxieties, resentments, unresolved tensions, hidden animosities and long-standing frustrations. Our spontaneous reaction to all is to run away and get busy again so that we at least can make ourselves believe that things are not as bad as they seem in our solitude.

> *Pause*

> The truth is that things are bad, even worse than they seem. It is this painful stripping away of the old self, this falling away from all our old support systems that enables us to cry out for the unconditional mercy of God. When we do not run away in fear, but patiently stay with our struggles, the outer space of solitude gradually becomes an inner space, a space in our hearts where we come to know the presence of the Spirit who has already been given to us.

Song
"A Place to Go" from *Calm Is the Night,* by the Monks of Weston Priory

Silence

Spontaneous Prayer

Closing

As we close our prayer, Lord, we ask for help to be faithful to you by spending some of our time each day in personal prayer. Help us also to be faithful to ourselves by taking advantage of the grace and knowledge obtained through prayer. Amen.

TESTAMENT THREADS:

Light of the World

Suggestion
Have several candles burning during this prayer session.

Opening
We open our prayer, Christ, remembering your words,

> "Walk while you have the [light],
> or darkness will come over you." (John 12:35b)

Song
"The Lord Is My Light" from *A Dwelling Place*, by the St. Louis Jesuits

> *Pause*

Readings
John 8:12:
"I am the light of the world.
No follower of mine shall ever walk in darkness;
no, he shall possess the light of life."

> *Pause*

Luke 11:33-36:
"One who lights a lamp does not put it in the cellar or under a bushel basket, but rather on a lampstand, so that they who come in may see the light. The eye is the lamp of your body. When your eyesight is sound, your whole body is lighted up, but when your eyesight is bad, your body is in darkness. Take care, then, that your light is not darkness. If your whole body is lighted up and not partly in darkness, it will be as fully illumined as when a lamp shines brightly for you."

Pause

John 9:5:
"While I am in the world
I am the light of the world."

Pause

Matthew 6:22-23:
"The eye is the body's lamp. If your eyes are good, your body will
be filled with light; if your eyes are bad, your body will be in
darkness. And if your light is darkness, how deep will the darkness
be!"

Pause

John 1:4-5:
Whatever came to be in him, found life,
life for the light of men.
The light shines on in darkness,
a darkness that did not overcome it.

Pause

John 1:9:
The real light which gives light to every man was coming into the
world.

Pause

John 3:19b-21:
"[T]he light came into the world,
but men loved darkness rather than light
because their deeds were wicked.
Everyone who practices evil
hates the light;
he does not come near it
for fear his deeds will be exposed.
But he who acts in truth
comes into the light,
to make clear
that his deeds are done in God."

Pause

John 12:46:
"I have come to the world as its light,

to keep anyone who believes in me
from remaining in the dark."

Pause

John 12:35-36:
Jesus answered:
"The light is among you only a little longer.
Walk while you still have it
or darkness will come over you.
The man who walks in the dark
does not know where he is going.
While you have the light,
keep faith in the light;
thus you will become sons of light."

Pause

Matthew 5:14-16:
"You are the light of the world. A city set on a hill cannot be
hidden. Men do not light a lamp and then put it under a bushel
basket. They set it on a stand, where it gives light to all in the
house. In the same way, your light must shine before men so that
they may see goodness in your acts and give praise to your heavenly
Father."

Pause

Song
"Nature and Grace" from *No Longer Strangers*, by John Michael
Talbot

Suggestion
If possible, have each person hold a candle during the silence and
spontaneous prayer.

Silence

Spontaneous Prayer

Closing
Blow out the candles and sing the Great Amen.

Friendship

Opening
We begin our prayer in the spirit of friendship. Let us close our eyes and take a minute to savor the support of fellowship we feel within this prayer group and with others who are close to us.

Song
"When With a Friend" from *Calm Is the Night,* by the Monks of Weston Priory

First Reading
Colossians 3:12-16 ("Put on love.")

Silence

Second Reading
John 13:34-35 ("Love one another.")

Pause

Third Reading
1 Thessalonians 4:9-12 (Love and labor)

Pause

Fourth Reading
John 15:12-17 ("You are my friends.")

Pause

Song
"Betwixt Me and My Brother" from *The God of Life,* by John Michael Talbot

Suggestion
Stand in a circle and hold hands during spontaneous prayer.

Spontaneous Prayer

Closing
In the spirit of friendship, let us close our prayer with a sign of peace—a hug, a handshake or a kiss.

Practicing the Presence of God

Opening
Let us begin in the name of God.

Song
"Only in God" from *A Dwelling Place*, by the St. Louis Jesuits

Reading
Psalm 139:1-18 (God is everywhere.)

> *Pause*

Commentary
During mundane chores as well as in our most passionate moments, God is with us. All we have to do is grow in our awareness of his presence. Even while we sin, God is right there, waiting for us to remember him. That "great awareness" is the practice of the presence of God which leads to a grace-filled life.

Brother Lawrence, a simple monk who devoted his life to fulfilling God's will in everything, gives us this advice in *The Practice of the Presence of God:*

> Our thoughts spoil everything. All the trouble begins with them. We must be careful to reject them as soon as we see that they are neither necessary to our occupation at the moment nor conducive to our salvation, and return to our communion with God, wherein is our only good.

> *Pause*

Meditation Exercise
Lord, help us to erase everything from our minds but you. We ask the Holy Spirit to still our thoughts so that we may come into communion with you.

> *Pause*

Close your eyes. Say the word "God" over and over again, once as you inhale and once as you exhale. Picture a circle in your mind's eye. The circle can be any color—a circle of light, of gold, of silver, even black—whatever comes into your mind's eye most easily. Hold that circle and keep repeating the word "God" as you breathe in and the word "God" as you breathe out. Don't be upset with yourself when your thoughts wander; just return your attention to the circle and the word "God."

Silence

Song
"God" from *The God of Life*, by John Michael Talbot

Silence

Spontaneous Prayer

Closing
We close our prayer in the name of God. Amen.

Turning the Other Cheek

Song
"Few Be the Lovers of the Cross" from *No Longer Strangers*, by John Michael Talbot

Opening
Speak to us, Lord. Help us listen to your Word and to enjoy being silent in each other's presence.

The theme of this prayer is turning the other cheek. You will each have the opportunity to share aloud what the Scripture reading meant to you, so please listen attentively and allow the Scripture to speak to you personally.

Pause

Lord, free us from anxiety and fear so that we may open our ears and our hearts to your Word.

Pause

First Reading
Matthew 5:38-48 (Turning the other cheek)

Silence

Instructions

Each person may now share aloud what the Scripture meant to him or her. The sharing is intended to be a reflection of personal experience, not a sermon for others. Keep comments short—just a few sentences. This sharing should not turn into a discussion. Be at ease with the silent gaps between comments.

Sharing

The same passage will be read aloud again. As you listen to it this time, reflect on the comments each person shared with the group.

Second Reading

Matthew 5:38-48

Instructions

There will be a period of silence and then spontaneous prayer. The prayers spoken aloud should relate to the reading and its effect on you. For example, "Father, give me the courage to turn the other cheek," or, "Jesus, thank you for speaking to us."

Silence

Spontaneous Prayer

Closing Song

"Peace to You" from *Calm Is the Night,* by the Monks of Weston Priory

Sharing Aids

If needed, the following questions may spark more sharing, and can be used by the leader during the first round of sharing.

1) Is "turning the other cheek" a recurring theme in the gospel or just another of those mysterious utterances of Jesus that is too unworldly for us to apply in real life?

2) At what times should we not turn the other cheek?

3) Tolstoy wrote at length on the verse, "Do not resist evil." He reasoned that to counter a strong, violent force with another strong, violent force was to empower each violence with more force. In other words, resistance empowers evil while nonresistance neutralizes or dissipates it.

cycle 4

SCRIPTURE THEME:

Happiness

Opening

As we begin our prayer, let us put away all dark and negative thoughts so that we may be flooded with the happiness which comes from God.

> *Pause*

Song

"Happy Man" from *Calm Is the Night*, by the Monks of Weston Priory

First Reading

Sirach 30:21-27 (Happiness)

> *Pause*

Second Reading

From *My Way of Life*, by Thomas Aquinas:

> Surely, then, we must say that man's happiness is to be found in the good of his soul. And in a way this is true. But just as the hunter must be more wary as he approaches nearer to his quarry, so we must be most careful as we come nearer to the end of our quest, the definition of real happiness. Obviously, happiness is not the soul itself; if it were all men would be happy from the beginning. But this is contrary to all our experience. Nor is it some particular perfection of the soul, such as science or prudence or virtue. For these once again are particular goods, which always leave something further to be desired. No, the only object which can completely satisfy all human desire is the absolutely

universal good, which is outside man, even outside the whole created world. Nothing can satisfy man's will completely, except the universal good, which gives complete rest to his appetite; and this is to be found not in any creature but in God alone. Man's happiness, then, is to be found in the possession of God. Briefly, God is the ultimate object, the ultimate end of all man's desires and the possesion of God by the soul is happiness.

Silence

Third Reading
Psalm 1 (True happiness)

Song
"Alleluia, He Is Coming" from *Cry Hosanna*, by Fisherfolk

Silence

Spontaneous Prayer

Closing
In the happiness and joy that come from God alone, we end our prayer. Amen.

PSALM THEME:

Trust in God

Opening
Let us begin our prayer with trust in our hearts.

Pause

Song
"Trust in the Lord" from *A Dwelling Place*, by the St. Louis Jesuits

Pause

First Reading
Psalm 27 (Trust in God)

Silence

Second Reading
Psalm 62 (Trust in God alone)

Silence

Third Reading
Psalm 145:14-21 (The Lord upholds us.)

Pause

Song
"Fill My Cup, Lord" from *Cry Hosanna*, by Fisherfolk

Silence

Spontaneous Prayer

Closing
Everyone gather in a circle, join hands and say the Lord's Prayer together.

SCRIPTURE THEME:

Poverty

Opening
Let us enter into prayer by getting in touch with our own poverty.

Song
"Lady Poverty" from *No Longer Strangers*, by John Michael Talbot

First Reading
From *Think and Grow Rich*, by Napoleon Hill:

> The fear of poverty is, without doubt, the most destructive of the six basic fears. The six basic fears are poverty, criticism, ill health, lost love, old age and death. Poverty has been placed at the head of the list because it is the most difficult to master. The fear of poverty grew out of man's inherited tendency to prey upon his fellow man economically. Nearly all animals lower than man are motivated by instinct, but their capacity to think is limited, therefore, they prey upon one another physically. Man, with his superior sense of

intuition, with the capacity to think and to reason, does not eat his fellow man bodily; he gets more satisfaction out of "eating" him financially. Man is so avaricious that every conceivable law has been passed to safeguard him from his fellow man.

Silence

Second Reading
Luke 12:22-34 (Dependence on providence)

Silence

Song
Gospel Reading (lilies of the field) and "Praise to the Father" from *Calm Is the Night*, by the Monks of Weston Priory

Silence

Spontaneous Prayer

Closing
Lord, help us to master our fear of poverty and to let go of our grasping tendencies. Amen.

MEDITATION THEME:

Strife

Opening
Creator and loving Father, we ask you to surround us with your love and wisdom and to give us hope to deal with the strife that is present in our lives.

Song
"Trust in the Lord" from *A Dwelling Place*, by the St. Louis Jesuits

Reading
Psalm 77 (Crying aloud to God)

Pause

Meditation Exercise
A time of prayer is not always a time to dwell on God and spiritual

matters. Quite the contrary is true. By taking what is bothering you to God, you integrate your prayer life with your daily life. Talk to God just as you would to a friend who is sitting beside you. Don't worry about judgment for what you may have done. Bringing your problem to God invites divine mercy and compassion. It is only by turning away in times of need that you offend God.

Pause

Close your eyes now and pour your heart out to the Lord. When you finish, open your heart to receive his answer. It may be a look of love, words of counsel or an overwhelming feeling that you are surrounded with love and protection. Ask God questions if you please, but be very silent and still as you wait for the answer. As much as possible, put away selfishness and your own will as you ask counsel from the Lord. After all, the more empty you are, the more God can fill you.

Pause

Song
"Flowers Still Grow There" from *Wood Hath Hope*, by John Foley, S. J.

Silence

Spontaneous Prayer

Closing
Help us to cope with strife by growing in awareness of the divine presence which surrounds us. We close our prayer, asking for the grace of awareness. Amen.

SCRIPTURE THEME:

Wisdom and Wealth

Opening
Let us begin our prayer in the name of God, who is "the guide of Wisdom/and the director of the wise" (Wisdom 7:15).

Song
"Your Love is Changing the World" from *Cry Hosanna,* by
Fisherfolk

First Reading
Luke 12:13-21 (The rich fool)

> *Pause*

Second Reading
From *The Song of the Bird,* by Anthony de Mello, S. J.:

> The wise man reached the outskirts of the village and
> settled down under the tree for the night when a villager
> came running up to him and said, "The stone! The stone!
> Give me the precious stone!"
>
> "What stone?" asked the wise man.
>
> "Last night an angel appeared to me in a dream,"
> said the villager, "and told me that if I went to the
> outskirts of the village at dusk I should find a wise man
> who would give me a precious stone that would make
> me rich forever."
>
> The wise man rummaged in his bag and pulled out
> a stone. "He probably meant this one," he said, as he
> handed the stone over to the villager. "I found it on a
> forest path some days ago. You can certainly have it."
>
> The man looked at the stone in wonder. It was a
> diamond. Probably the largest diamond in the whole
> world for it was as large as a man's head.
>
> He took the diamond and walked away. All night
> he tossed about in bed, unable to sleep. Next day at
> the crack of dawn he woke the wise man and said, "Give
> me the wealth that makes it possible for you to give
> this diamond away so easily."

> *Pause*

Third Reading
Matthew 13:44 (Hidden treasure)

Song
"Lady Poverty" from *No Longer Strangers,* by John Michael Talbot

> *Silence*

> *Spontaneous Prayer*

Closing

God, give us the wisdom to recognize true wealth in our day-to-day routine. Amen.

Discipline

Opening

As we focus on the theme of discipline, help us, Lord, to see the connection between the words *disciple* and *discipline*.

Song

"Lose Yourself in Me" from *I Will Not Forget You*, by Carey Landry

Instructions

While reading the following phrases, play the song "Lose Yourself in Me" again, but turn the volume very low. When the song finishes, allow the next one, "Brother Jesus," to play through, too.

Readings

Proverbs 3:11-12:
The discipline of the LORD, my son, disdain not;
    spurn not his reproof;
For whom the Lord loves he reproves,
    and he chastises the son he favors.

> *Pause*

Deuteronomy 4:36:
Out of the heavens he let you hear his voice to discipline you; on earth he let you see his great fire, and you heard him speaking out of the fire.

> *Pause*

Hebrews 12:5b-6:
"My sons, do not disdain the discipline of the Lord
    nor lose heart when he reproves you;
For whom the Lord loves, he disciplines;
    he scourges every son he receives."

> *Pause*

Hebrews 12:7:
Endure your trials as the discipline of God, who deals with you as sons. For what son is there whom his father does not discipline?

Pause

Proverbs 12:1 (RSV):
Whoever loves discipline, loves knowledge,
  but he who hates reproof is stupid.

Pause

Hebrews 12:9-10:
If we respected our earthly fathers who corrected us, should we not all the more submit to the Father of spirits, and live? They disciplined us as seemed right to them, to prepare us for the short span of mortal life; but God does so for our true profit, that we may share his holiness.

Pause

Colossians 3:5:
Put to death whatever in your nature is rooted in earth: fornication, uncleanness, passion, evil desires, and that lust which is idolatry.

Pause

Matthew 12:35-37:
"A good man produces good from his store of goodness; an evil man produces evil from his evil store. I assure you, on judgment day people will be held accountable for every unguarded word they speak. By your words you will be acquitted, and by your words you will be condemned."

Pause

Instructions
Allow the song "Brother Jesus" to finish.

Silence

Spontaneous Prayer

Closing
Let us close our prayer in gratitude for the bonds of discipleship. Amen.

Death

Opening

Realizing that death is but a doorway to a richer, fuller life, we open our prayer in memory of our deceased sister/brother_____.

Pause

Song

"Only in God" from *A Dwelling Place*, by the St. Louis Jesuits

First Reading

John 5:24-29 (Eternal life)

Pause

Second Reading

Psalm 39 (Life's brevity)

Pause

Third Reading

John 11:25-26 ("I am the resurrection and the life.")

Pause

Fourth Reading

1 Corinthians 15:51-58 (Victory over death)

Song

"Healer of My Soul" from *The God of Life*, by John Michael Talbot

Sharing Suggestion

In an attitude of rejoicing and celebration, share memories and feelings about the deceased. You will actually feel the presence of that person among you. After the informal sharing, offer your prayers.

Sharing

Spontaneous Prayer

Song

"A Place to Go" from *Calm Is the Night*, by the Monks of Weston Priory

Silence

Closing

We close our prayer with the reminder that death is hell to the soul that dies only once, but heaven to the soul that dies a little each day.

MEDITATION THEME:

Redeeming Our Shadow Side

Opening

Master of my soul, grant me the light to penetrate the dark, shadowy side of my psyche and grant me the grace to stand firm in the presence of my own iniquities.

Song

"Flowers Still Grow There" from *Wood Hath Hope*, by John Foley, S. J.

Readings

Job 3:20-26 (Job's plaint)

    Pause

John 15:1-5 (The vine and the branches)

    Pause

Meditation Exercise

Imagine the effect you would have on someone if you found them so utterly disgusting that you denied their very presence. How would that person feel? Would your behavior in any way lead the person to change or growth? Certainly not. It is the same with those parts of you that you don't want to own.

Like it or not, we are all part of that tree of human life which has its roots in the dark of the earth and its blossoms in the light of the sun.

How then do we deal with our savage, primitive roots—our cravings and violence? First of all, we must own up to that side of our nature and begin to treat it with tenderness and care rather than rejection. It is useless to spend time harboring guilt and shame over these currently unacceptable parts of ourselves. Rather, we must give our dark side light, understanding, patience and time. Progress may be slow, but eventually any passionate extreme can be harnessed with the bridle of love and discipline and end up serving as a powerful source of personal growth. This idea is summed up nicely in a graffiti verse I saw on a Denver sidewalk years ago:

> In the garden of life, remember that the compost is just as important as the harvest.

During the silent time, find in your subconscious one phantom that has been nagging at you and bring it to the surface. Accept this phantom, forgive any damage it may have done to you or others and then befriend it. By getting to know this dark aspect of yourself, you will discover your own hidden motivations. The more familiar you become with your shadow, the more you can redeem it and help it to occupy a productive place in your garden of life.

> *Silence*

Song
"Holy God of Truth" from *The God of Life*, by John Michael Talbot

> *Silence*

> *Spontaneous Prayer*

Closing
Help us grow to wholeness, Lord, by redeeming the rejected parts of our being. Amen.

COLLATIO:

The Adulteress

Song
"Nature and Grace" from *No Longer Strangers*, by John Michael Talbot

Opening
Speak to us, Lord. Help us to listen to your Word and to enjoy

being silent in each other's presence. As we will each have the opportunity to share aloud the meaning of the Scripture reading, let us listen attentively and allow the Scripture to speak to each of us personally.

Pause

Speak to us, Lord, through your Scripture.

Pause

First Reading
John 8:1-11 (The adulteress)

Silence

Instructions
Each person may now share aloud what the Scripture meant to him or her. The sharing is intended to be a reflection of personal experience, not a sermon for others. Keep comments short—just a few sentences. This sharing should not turn into discussion. Be at ease with the silent gaps between comments.

Sharing

Instructions
The same passage will be read aloud again. As you listen to it this time, reflect on the comments each person shared with the group.

Second Reading
John 8:1-11

Instructions
There will be a period of silence and then spontaneous prayer. The prayers spoken aloud should relate to the reading and its effect on you. For instance, "Divine Presence, remind me not to judge others but, rather, to look within," or, "Lord, heal me from my sins."

Silence

Spontaneous Prayer

Closing Song
"Brother Jesus" from *I Will Not Forget You,* by Carey Landry

Sharing Aids

If needed, the following questions may spark more sharing and can be used by the leader during the first round of sharing.

1) According to the Pharisees, Moses would have stoned the adulteress while Jesus does not even condemn her verbally. What accounts for this dramatic difference?

2) Someone once guessed that Jesus might have been writing each person's sins; that is why they all fled from the scene. What do you suppose he was writing in the sand?

cycle 5

'Blessed Are the Poor'

Opening
"Blest are you poor; the reign of God is yours" (Luke 6:20b).

Song
"Lady Poverty" from *No Longer Strangers*, by John Michael Talbot

First Reading
Matthew 6:19-21 (True riches)

>   *Pause*

Matthew 6:24 (Serve God or money.)

>   *Silence*

Second Reading
From *Call To Conversion*, by Jim Wallis:

> In the New Testament we find more than 500 verses of direct teaching about the rich and the poor. Jesus talked more about wealth and poverty than almost any other subject including heaven and hell, sexual morality, the law or violence.
>
> Wealth is seen, at best, as a great spiritual danger and, most often, as an absolute hindrance to trust in God. The rich are continually held responsible for the sufferings of the poor, while God is portrayed as the deliverer of the oppressed. The God of the Bible has taken sides on this matter and has emphatically chosen the side of the poor. Sharing with the poor is not regarded as an option but as the normal consequence of faith in God.

Third Reading
Mark 10:17-22 (The rich young man)

Silence

Fourth Reading
From *Call To Conversion*, by Jim Wallis:

> Jesus is God made poor. His coming was prophesied to bring social revolution and his kingdom would turn things upside down. The mighty would be brought low, the rich sent away empty, the poor exalted, the hungry satisfied (Luke 1:52-53). Jesus identified himself with the weak, the outcast, the downtrodden. His kingdom undermines all economic systems that reward the rich and punish the poor.

Song
"Cry of the Poor" from *Wood Hath Hope*, by John Foley, S. J.

Silence

Spontaneous Prayer

Closing Thought
"An Indian village, with all its poverty and squalor and disease, has still a sacred character, of which a modern suburb with all its affluence and cleanliness and health service has not a trace" (from *Return to the Center*, by Bede Griffith).

PSALM THEME:

Hope and Longing for God

Opening
Join hands and say the Lord's Prayer together. Then, during the silence that follows, say the Lord's Prayer slowly to yourself.

Silence

First Reading
Psalm 63 (Longing for God)

Pause

Song
"Come to the Water" from *Wood Hath Hope*, by John Foley, S. J.

Second Reading
Psalm 42 (Desire for God)

Silence

Third Reading
Psalm 130 (Waiting for God)

Pause

Song
"Peace is Flowing Like a River" from *I Will Not Forget You*, by Carey Landry

Silence

Spontaneous Prayer

Closing
Our prayer together is ended. Let us go forth in peace.

SCRIPTURE THEME:

Justice

Opening
Help us, Lord, to become worthy laborers in the fields of injustice.

Song
"Isaiah 58" from *No Longer Strangers*, by John Michael Talbot

First Reading
Isaiah 42:1-9 (The servant's mission)

Pause

Second Reading
James 5:1-6 (Warning to the oppressor)

Silence

Commentary

Injustice is everywhere. But each one of us can quietly stand up against it wherever we find it. We tend to be paralyzed by injustice because it is so firmly rooted in our systems. We do have the power, however, each in our own way, to champion the underdog or to root out injustice in a particular instance.

Sometimes this can be accomplished in conversation by merely taking a quiet stand (in a humble rather than in a preachy manner) against prejudice, hate or oppression.

Words have power. You'd be surprised at how much terms and tones of reconciliation, openness and fair play bring about justice and peace. If our actions then follow those same patterns by reaching out to the minority, the marginal, we have taken a big step in countering the injustice inherent in this world.

Silence

Song

"Holy God of Truth" from *The God of Life,* by John Michael Talbot

Silence

Spontaneous Prayer

Closing

God, we close our prayer, asking for the courage to confront injustice as we become aware of it in our surroundings. Amen.

MEDITATION THEME:

Music

Instructions for the Leader

Before you begin, ask the prayer participants to name two of their favorite songs from among those you have on record or tape.

Opening

"The LORD is my strength and my song" (Exodus 15:2, RSV). Our theme is music; let's begin by joining hands and saying or singing the Lord's Prayer.

Pause

Meditation Exercise

One of the most prayerful exercises I have ever experienced has been listening to the music from *Jesus Christ, Superstar*, particularly the song, "I Only Want to Say." Hearing that one song over and over again helped bring me face-to-face with Christ.

Listen now with your whole being to each of the following songs. Allow the words to come alive in your heart. Pick one particular phrase from each song that speaks to you. Turn the phrase over in your mind during the silent time and explore its implications for your life.

(For instance, if you listened to the "Servant Song" and selected the phrase, "Let me be your servant, let me be as Christ to you," just imagine how a conviction like that would revolutionize your relationships. How would you be Christ to those around you? If you listened to "Fill My Cup, Lord" and picked that title as the phrase, ask yourself what it would mean to have the Lord fill your cup. Would you take whatever the Lord poured out for you? If the cup were bitter, would you ask that it be removed?)

Play one song.

> *Silence*

Play another song.

> *Silence*

> *Spontaneous Prayer*

Closing

Join hands and sing the Great Amen.

SCRIPTURE THEME:

Guardian Angels

Opening

During tonight's prayer, God, give me the freedom to open up so that I might receive the direction and help that my guardian angel is waiting to give me.

Song
"For We Are Free" from *Calm Is the Night*, by the Monks of Weston Priory

First Reading
Exodus 23:20-22 ("I send an angel before you.")

     Pause

Second Reading
Psalm 91:9-13 ("He will give his angels charge over you.")

     Pause

Third Reading
Luke 1:8-20 (Gabriel appears to Zechariah.)

     Pause

Fourth Reading
Luke 1:26-36 (Gabriel appears to Mary.)

     Pause

Commentary
Few people realize the power they have to draw on in the form of their guardian angel—that higher force or guide that is assigned to each person at birth. This ally counteracts our selfish and wild tendencies. The more aware we become of our heavenly benefactor, the more we can channel its help and direction within our lives.

Confer with this valuable associate in all of your dealings. Ask for advice and guidance in your decisions. Since the purpose of your guardian angel is to assist you in reaching your lifetime goal, this close friend should be sought particularly at those times in your life when you are contemplating a change, beginning a new project, selecting a mate, etc.

Instructions
Take a few minutes now to open up the channel between you and your guardian angel. Ask for assistance in getting in touch with God's will for you and listen to the angel's answer.

     Silence

Song

"When With a Friend" from *Calm Is the Night,* by the Monks of
Weston Priory

Silence

Spontaneous Prayer

Closing

Our prayer is ended. Let us go forth with the knowledge that our
guide is always there and is ever ready to act creatively to bring
about God's will for us. Amen.

TESTAMENT THREADS:

Reign of God

Opening

Let us relax a minute and become aware of the presence of God
within us and around us.

Song

"God" from *The God of Life,* by John Michael Talbot

Readings

Luke 17:20-22:

Once, on being asked by the Pharisees when the reign of God
would come, [Jesus] replied: "You cannot tell by careful watching
when the reign of God will come. Neither is it a matter of reporting
that it is 'here' or 'there.' The reign of God is already in your midst."

Pause

Luke 13:18b-19:

"What does the reign of God resemble? To what shall I liken it?
It is like a mustard seed which a man took and planted in his
garden. It grew and became a large shrub and the birds of the air
nested in its branches."

Pause

Luke 13:20b-21:

"To what shall I compare the reign of God? It is like yeast which a woman took to knead into three measures of flour until the whole mass of dough began to rise."

Pause

Luke 18:16b-17:
"Let the little children come to me. Do not shut them off. The reign of God belongs to such as these. Trust me when I tell you that whoever does not accept the kingdom of God as a child will not enter into it."

Pause

Luke 21:34-36:
"Be on guard lest your spirits become bloated with indulgence and drunkenness and worldly cares. The great day will suddenly close in on you like a trap. The day I speak of will come upon all who dwell on the face of the earth. So be on the watch. Pray constantly for the strength to escape whatever is in prospect, and to stand secure before the Son of Man."

Pause

Song
"We Go On Waiting" from *Calm Is the Night*, by the Monks of Weston Priory

Silence

Spontaneous Prayer

Closing
Join hands and pray the Our Father together.

SCRIPTURE THEME:

Love

Opening
The theme of this prayer session is love. Jesus tells us to love our neighbors as ourselves, but even as far back as Leviticus, the third book of the Old Testament, we find the instruction:

Take no revenge and cherish no grudge against your

fellow countrymen. You shall love your neighbor as yourself. (Leviticus 19:18)

Song
"Your Love Is Changing the World" from *Cry Hosanna*, by Fisherfolk

First Reading
1 John 3:16-18 (Love in action)

> *Pause*

Second Reading
1 Corinthians 13:1-8 (The nature of love)

> *Pause*

Commentary
Love does not demonstrate itself through feelings, words or thoughts. No, the decision to love is made in the will and, once made, is then nicely expressed through emotions and language. If you want to know whom or what a person loves, look at where the person spends her or his time and energy. Just as the fox said to the Little Prince, "It is the time you have wasted on your rose that makes it so important," you too paint a portrait of your love with the strokes of time and the coloration of energy.

> *Pause*

Third Reading
John 13:34-35 (The new commandment)

> *Silence*

Song
"Brother Jesus" from *I Will Not Forget You*, by Carey Landry

> *Silence*

> *Spontaneous Prayer*

Closing
Our prayer is ended. Let us go forth as channels of God's love. Amen.

Kingdom of God Within You

Opening

Lord, we ask you to quiet our minds and still our bodies so that we may hear your words not only with our ears but in our hearts.

Song

"A Place to Go" from *Calm Is the Night*, by the Monks of Weston Priory

First Reading

Luke 17:21 (The kingdom of God)

>*Pause*

Second Reading

Psalm 51:6-12 (A clean heart)

>*Pause*

Meditation Exercise

Close your eyes and go within yourself to find God. Still your body and thoughts. Concentrate on picturing your heart in your mind's eye. See how your heart moves with the rhythm of your breath. Imagine that your heart grows bigger and bigger and takes over your whole body. Your heart is the seat of love, mercy and compassion, so love, mercy and compassion take over your whole body. Your heart is the seat of God, so God takes over your whole body. Rest in this image.

>*Silence*

Song

"God" from *The God of Life*, by John Michael Talbot

>*Silence*

>*Spontaneous Prayer*

Closing

We close with a phrase we have prayed over before: "Be still and know that I am God" (Psalm 46:10, RSV). Amen.

Lilies of the Field

Song
"Trust in the Lord" from *A Dwelling Place*, by the St. Louis Jesuits

Opening
Speak to us Lord. Help us listen to your Word and to enjoy being silent in each other's presence. As we will each have the opportunity to share aloud the meaning of the Scripture reading, let us listen attentively and allow the Scripture to speak to each of us personally.

Pause

First Reading
Matthew 6:25-34 (Lilies of the field)

Silence

Instructions
Each person may now share aloud what the Scripture meant to him or her. The sharing is intended to be a reflection of personal experience, not a sermon for others. Keep comments short—just a few sentences. This sharing should not turn into discussion. Be at ease with the silent gaps between comments.

Sharing

Instructions
The same passage will be read aloud again. As you listen to it this time, reflect on the comments each person shared with the group.

Second Reading
Matthew 6:25-34

Instructions
There will be a period of silence and then spontaneous prayer. The prayers spoken aloud should relate to the reading and its effect on you. For example, "Father, ease my anxious heart," or "Help me to let go of the things of this world, God, and seek your kingdom."

Silence

Spontaneous Prayer

Closing Song
"Fill My Cup, Lord" from *Cry Hosanna*, by Fisherfolk

Sharing Aids
If needed, the following questions may spark more sharing and
can be used by the leader during the first round of sharing.

1) Which practices in our current-day economic system
conflict with this Scripture passage?

2) Do you think that if you took this Scripture passage to
heart and practiced it, you and your family would be
poverty-stricken?

3) Gandhi said that there was enough in the world to meet
each person's need but not enough to meet each person's greed.
Are we working so hard to meet our needs or to hang on to our
luxuries?

cycle 6

Mary and Martha

Opening
Let us begin in the name of God our Father.

Song
"Servant Song" from *Cry Hosanna*, by Fisherfolk

>   *Pause*

Reading
Luke 10:38-42 (Martha and Mary)

>   *Pause*

Commentary
There are many different interpretations to this story, but one excellent insight that it leaves with us is the realization of the futility of too much busyness—something that many of Jesus' most ardent disciples get caught up in. For many of us busyness is compulsive behavior, a form of greed as we chalk up marks on our spiritual scoreboards. We want to do so much for God that we don't have the time to take a moment to look into the divine heart and find out what God wants us to do. Really, we don't have to do nearly as much as we think. Most important is probably letting go or surrendering our will to God's will. Martha was so busy rushing around serving Jesus that she did not have the presence of mind to realize that all he wanted was a simple meal and some loving friendship.

The difficulty with helping others is that we usually want to help them in the way we determine they should be helped rather than the way *they* want to be helped. We make our judgments of what we think is best for them rather than allowing them the dignity and freedom to choose what they want from us. Mary took the time to know and understand what Jesus needed while, at the same time, she accepted the words of life that he had to give her. This is why Mary chose the better part.

Silence

Song

"Hail Mary: Gentle Woman" from *I Will Not Forget You*, by Carey Landry

Silence

Spontaneous Prayer

Closing

Our prayer together is ended. Let us go forth in peace to serve one another.

PSALM THEME:

Guardian and Shepherd

Opening

Let us begin our prayer in the name of Jesus, our Shepherd.

Song

"Like a Shepherd" from *A Dwelling Place*, by the St. Louis Jesuits

Readings

Psalm 23 ("The Lord is my shepherd.")

Silence

Psalm 138 (Hymn of thanks)

Silence

Psalm 121 (The Lord, our guardian)

Pause

Song

"I Lift Up My Eyes" from *Calm Is the Night,* by the Monks of Weston Priory

Silence

Spontaneous Prayer

Closing
We close our prayer, giving thanks to the Lord, our guardian and shepherd. Amen.

SCRIPTURE THEME:

Humility

Opening
Let us begin our prayer to the Father in the spirit of humility by taking a moment of silence to thank God for all he has given us.

Song
"The Servant Song" from *Cry Hosanna*, by Fisherfolk

First Reading
1 Peter 5:5-11 ("Humble yourself.")

Pause

Second Reading
Luke 18:9-14 (The Pharisee and the tax collector)

Pause

Third Reading
Philippians 2:1-4 (Imitating Christ's humility)

Pause

Suggestion
During the silent period, you might try to open yourself up to a greater awareness of what humility means.

Humility is a word we toss around a lot. We hear it and use it in church but forget about it completely when someone barges ahead of us in the church parking lot. How often do we let the other person go first? How often do we rejoice at someone's success rather than feel jealous? I remember reading in some spiritual classic years ago that we know when we are growing in goodness when we cease to feel pleased when something bad happens to someone else. We seldom admit this, even to ourselves, but if you look deeply it is there in most of us— smugness when something goes wrong for someone else—a sense of superiority which puts us on top.

Where is humility working in your life now and where is it absent?

Silence

Fourth Reading
1 Corinthians 4:6-13 (The humility of the apostles)

Song
"Peace Prayer" from *A Dwelling Place,* by the St. Louis Jesuits

Silence

Share insights on humility if you like along with your spontaneous prayer.

Spontaneous Prayer and Sharing

Closing
Our prayer is over. Let us go humbly to find Christ in others. Amen.

MEDITATION THEME:

Emptying Our Hearts to the Lord

Opening
We begin our prayer by emptying our hearts of everything but the presence of the Spirit within us.

Pause

Song
"For We Are Free" from *Calm Is the Night,* by the Monks of Weston Priory

Reading
Matthew 6:5-6 (How to pray)

Pause

Meditation Exercise

A preacher once asked his congregation what they would do if Christ walked down the aisle. The answer was that everyone would get very busy. Why is it that when we are busy we *think* we are good? The truth is our busyness often hides the bitterness and resentment in our heart. Rather than being so busy on the outside, it is equally important to be busy within: to look into our hearts and become aware of our motivations, our compulsions and our gifts.

Close your eyes now and empty your hearts of your day-to-day cares. Feel the divine presence growing within you. When thoughts and worries distract you, raise them to the Lord. Tell him about your concerns and ask him about your motivations. Then be silent. Listen for his answer. Wait for his light and consolation.

Pause

Reading

Read again the first reading—Matthew 6:5-6.

Silence

Song

"Peace Prayer" from *A Dwelling Place*, by the St. Louis Jesuits

Suggestion for Spontaneous Prayer

Since the meditation exercise was conversing with the Lord, try to share some of that experience and express your gratefulness during the time of spontaneous prayer. For example, "Lord, thank you for helping me accept responsibility for the problem I brought to you," or "Father, thank you for your mercy and compassion with me. I pray that I may treat others in the same way."

Spontaneous Prayer

Closing

Our prayer is ended. Let us go forth in peace. Amen.

Dreams: The Divine Language

Opening

The theme of this prayer is "Dreams: The Divine Language." We open our prayer with a quotation from the Old Testament:

"[I]n dreams will I speak to him" (Numbers 12:6b).

Pause

Song

"Calm Is the Night" from *Calm Is the Night,* by the Monks of Weston Priory

First Reading

Genesis 28:10-22 (Jacob's Dream)

Pause

Commentary

Dreams do seem to be a way God has of communicating with us. In the Old Testament there are 16 references to dreams; in the New Testament there are four or five.

Louis M. Savary, Patricia Berne and Stephan Williams, authors of *Dreams and Spiritual Growth,* encourage each one of us to use our nocturnal messages and visions for spiritual growth, "It is our fundamental premise that we gain more from dreams by doing things in response to them than we do from simply interpreting them." When you have a dream that seems significant to you, ask yourself the following questions:

What is the dream asking of me?
What issues in my life or in myself is this dream raising for me?
How am I going to respond to this dream?

Notice in the Scripture that we already read and in the passage we are about to read that both Jacob and Joseph responded to and used the knowledge they received in their dreams.

Pause

Second Reading

Matthew 1:18-25 (Joseph's Dream)

Pause

Song

"Healer of My Soul" from *The God of Life,* by John Michael Talbot

Silence

Spontaneous Prayer

Closing

We close our prayer with the Psalmist's words: "[The LORD] give to his beloved in sleep."

Divine Love

Opening

Let us open our prayer by surrendering ourselves to the call of unconditional love.

Song

"Your Love Is Changing the World" from *Cry Hosanna,* by Fisherfolk

Readings

Psalm 130:6:
My soul waits for the LORD
  more than sentinels wait for the dawn.

Pause

Psalm 4:7b:
O LORD, let the light of your countenance shine upon us!

Pause

Psalm 23:1:
The LORD is my shepherd; I shall not want.

Pause

Psalm 27:1a:
The LORD is my light and my salvation;
  whom should I fear?

Pause

Psalm 27:7:
Hear, O LORD, the sound of my call;
    have pity on me, and answer me.

Pause

John 14:13-14:
"...[W]hatever you ask in my name,
I will do,
so as to glorify the Father in the Son.
Anything you ask me in my name
I will do."

Pause

John 14:18:
"I will not leave you orphaned.
I will come back to you."

Pause

Isaiah 42:16:
I will lead the blind in their journey;
    by paths unknown I will guide them.

Pause

Isaiah 43:1:
Fear not for I have redeemed you;
    I have called you by name: you are mine.

Pause

Suggestion
While listening to the music and during the silent time, reflect on
the thought that divine love is unconditional; it is always there
waiting for our response.

Song
"Betwixt Me and My Brother" from *The God of Life*, by John
Michael Talbot

Silence

Spontaneous Prayer

Closing

We end our prayer praising your divinity and love. Amen.

God as Father

Opening

We begin our prayer in the name of God our Father.

Song

"Litany," "Healing Prayer" and "The Lord's Prayer" from *Calm Is the Night,* by the Monks of Weston Priory

First Reading

Matthew 11:25-27 (Jesus reveals the Father.)

Pause

Second Reading

From *God's Word Today*:

> We find it natural to think of God as our Father and to pray to him as our Father but we are able to do this only because of Jesus Christ. What we do naturally and unthinkingly in fact represents a radical development in the relationship between God and his people, a change made by and in Jesus.
>
> The fatherhood of God is occasionally mentioned in the Old Testament. Jesus, however, constantly referred to God as his Father. The Gospels contain about 170 occurrences of Jesus praying to God as his Father or speaking of God as his Father. Except for opening words of Psalm 22 prayed from the cross, every prayer of Jesus recorded in the Gospels is explicitly addressed to God as Father.
>
> Jesus not only addressed God as Father, he spoke of him as *"my Father."* The few Old Testament texts that spoke of God's fatherhood generally referred to God as the Father of the whole chosen people. Jesus, in contrast, spoke of and prayed to God as his own particular Father. In fact, Jesus was accused of

blasphemy because he spoke of God this way (see John 5:18).

Jesus went even further. In Aramaic, Jesus' native language, the word *abba* is the form of address a young child would use to address his or her father. Jesus addressed God as his *Abba*—almost as "Daddy." His prayers addressed God in very familiar and affectionate terms. Jesus prayed to Yahweh not as a distant Father but as a close and loving "*Abba*."

Third Reading
Galatians 4:1-7 (Heirs to the Father's kingdom)

Song
"Father, Make Me Holy" from *The God of Life*, by John Michael Talbot

Silence

Spontaneous Prayer

Closing
Join hands and say the Our Father together.

MEDITATION THEME:

Our Father

Opening
We open our prayer in the name of our heavenly Father.

Song
"Father, Make Me Holy" from *The God of Life*, by John Michael Talbot

Reading
Matthew 6:5-14 (The Lord's Prayer)

Pause

Meditation Exercise
Down through the centuries many of the saints and mystics have aspired to communion with God by practicing this simple form of

prayer (its very simplicity is what makes it so powerful!): Begin by saying the Lord's Prayer silently to yourself. Concentrate on each word and focus all of your attention on the prayer you are saying. When your mind wanders and you find yourself thinking of something other than the prayer, go back to the prayer at the point where you lost your concentration. Each time you finish the prayer, start it over again.

You can practice this form of prayer for five minutes, 10 minutes or hours at a time. You can practice it while you wait in line at the supermarket or while you are in the dentist's chair.

Close your eyes now and begin to say the Lord's Prayer to yourself. Say it slowly and give each word your full attention.

Silence

Songs
"Litany," "Healing" and "Lord's Prayer" from *Calm Is the Night,* by the Monks of Weston Priory

Pause

Spontaneous Prayer

Closing
Join hands and pray the Our Father together.

COLLATIO:

God's Requirements for Holiness

Song
"God" from *The God of Life,* by John Michael Talbot

Opening
The theme of our prayer is "God's Requirements for Holiness." You will each have the opportunity to share aloud what the Scripture reading meant to you, so please listen attentively and allow the Scripture to speak to you personally.

Pause

Lord, free us from anxiety and fear so that we may open our ears and our hearts to your Word.

Pause

First Reading
Isaiah 1:10-17 (God's requirements for a holy life)

Silence

Instructions
Each person may now share aloud what the Scripture meant to him or her. The sharing is intended to be a reflection of personal experience, not a sermon for others. Keep comments short—just a few sentences. This sharing should not turn into discussion. Be at ease with the silent gaps between comments.

Sharing

Instructions
The same passage will be read aloud again. As you listen to it this time, reflect on the comments each person shared with the group.

Second Reading
Isaiah 1:10-17

Instructions
There will be a period of silence and then spontaneous prayer. The prayer spoken aloud should relate to the reading and its effect on you. For example, "Father, help me to seek justice and end oppression," or, "God, give me the freedom to serve you in your way, not my way."

Silence

Spontaneous Prayer

Closing Song
"The Cry of the Poor" from *Wood Hath Hope*, by John Foley, S.J.

Sharing Aids
If needed, the following questions may spark more sharing and can be used by the leader during the first round of sharing.

1) Does God tire of our praise of him?

2) What is the right balance between praise of God and service to one's neighbor?

cycle 7

SCRIPTURE THEME:

'Many Are Called; Few Are Chosen'

Opening

Let us open our prayer with a minute of silence so that we may grow in awareness of the gift of God's grace.

Silence

Song

"Nature and Grace" from *No Longer Strangers*, by John Michael Talbot

First Reading

Matthew 22:1-14 (Many are called but few are chosen.)

Pause

Second Reading

From *The Road Less Traveled*, by M. Scott Peck:

> I have come to believe and have tried to demonstrate that people's capacity to love, and hence their will to grow, is nurtured not only by the love of their parents during childhood but also throughout their lives by grace, or God's love.

Pause

> It is because of grace that it is possible for people who have had loveless parents to become themselves loving individuals who rise far above their parents on the scale of human evolution. Why then do only some people spiritually grow and evolve beyond circumstances of their parentage? I believe that grace is available to everyone and that we are all cloaked in the love of God,

no one less nobly than another. The only answer I can give, therefore, is that most of us choose not to heed the call of grace and to reject its assistance.

Pause

Christ's assertion "Many are called but few are chosen," I would translate to mean "All of us are called by and to grace, but few of us choose to listen to the call."

Pause

To be aware of grace, to experience personally its constant presence, to know one's nearness to God, is to know and continually experience an inner tranquility and peace that few possess.

Song
"Peace Is Flowing Like a River" from *I Will Not Forget You*, by Carey Landry

Silence

Spontaneous Prayer

Closing
Our prayer together is ended. Help us, Holy Spirit, to respond to the gift of grace. Amen.

PSALM THEME:

Giving Thanks

Opening
We open our prayer, giving thanks to God and grateful for the beauty of creation and the abundance that surrounds us.

Song
"Your Love Is Changing the World" from *Cry Hosanna*, by Fisherfolk.

First Reading
Psalm 116 (Thanksgiving)

Silence

Second Reading
Psalm 118 (Thanks to the Lord)

Pause

Song
"Thanks to Thee" from *The God of Life*, by John Michael Talbot

Silence

Spontaneous Prayer

Suggestion
During the silent time and spontaneous prayer, form a circle either on the floor or around a table and hold hands while offering spontaneous prayers of thanks. Try to be silent for at least five minutes so that you can really come alive with gratefulness.

Closing
Father, we thank you for this chance to come together with each other to give thanks to you. Amen.

SCRIPTURE THEME:

Lifting Our Souls to the Divine

Opening
Let us open our prayer with a few minutes of silence to lift our souls to the divine.

Silence

Song
"I Lift Up My Soul" from *A Dwelling Place*, by the St. Louis Jesuits

First Reading
Psalm 25 ("To you I lift up my soul.")

Silence

Second Reading
Revelation 21:1-8 (New heavens and new earth)

Pause

Third Reading

Meister Eckhart, as quoted in *Breakthrough*, by Matthew Fox, says this about lifting our souls to the divine:

> To find in oneself the place of God, the soul must be lifted above all thoughts concerned with things. It will not succeed in this if it does not rid itself of the passions which, through thought, tie it to worldly things. It will rid itself of passions by means of the virtues and of simple thoughts by means of spiritual knowledge. It will leave this spiritual knowledge in turn when that light appears which, at the hour of prayer, forms the place of God.

Silence

Song

"I Lift Up My Eyes" from *Calm Is the Night*, by the Monks of Weston Priory

Suggestion

During this silent time, lift your thoughts from your earthly needs and concentrate on spiritual knowledge. Put all worldly cares aside and concentrate on the divine. When you find you are distracted in prayer, gently ask the distractions to depart and lift your thoughts to God again.

Silence

Spontaneous Prayer

Closing

Our prayer together is ended. Let us go forth, eager to see the divine in everything around us. Amen.

Mother of Creation

Opening

We open our prayer in honor of that feminine, creative presence in each of us.

Song

"Hail Mary: Gentle Woman" from *I Will Not Forget You*, by Carey Landry

First Reading

Wisdom 7:24-30 (The nature of Wisdom)

Pause

Second Reading

From "Prayer to the Forgotten Divine Mother," by Sister Francis B. Rothluebber, O.S.F., from *Praying*:

> The human family needs to return to you, Divine
>> Mother.
> The way to find you
>> is to go quietly before dawn
>> to an inner shoreline
>> of absolute, exquisite stillness.
>> At the movement of the Divine Breath over the night
>>> waters
>> we know your presence
>> around us and within us
>> pouring life into all living.
>
> Mother, Breath of all living,
>> awaken us to a new sense of power,
>> true power that shares in your life-giving energy
>> that is not power-over, domination nor violation
>> of the earth, of space, of each other.
>> Teach us the power of reverent creative love.
>
> The human family needs to return to you, Divine
>> Mother.
> The way to find you
>> is to sit watching a flower open

in unhurried quiet.
In the hidden working of your wisdom,
the conscious love directing growth inside each being
we know your presence.

Sophia, Wisdom creating from within,
encourage us to trust you, our Inner Teacher
Let us taste your spontaneity and delight
in the unexpected way of your wisdom
guiding us to our full life.

Pause

Meditation Exercise
Go to your own inner shoreline. Sit comfortably along the water
and block out all thoughts and sounds except the sound of the
water. When you have achieved stillness, look down the shoreline.
The Mother of creation is approaching you. She has something to
say to you. What is it?

Silence

Song
"Flowers Still Grow There" from *Wood Hath Hope*, by John Foley,
S. J.

Closing
Amen.

SCRIPTURE THEME:

Unity

Opening
To begin our prayer, let us reach out to one another, join hands
and pray together as sisters and brothers to our heavenly Father:
"Our Father, who art in heaven...."

Pause

Song
"One Bread, One Body" from *Wood Hath Hope*, by John Foley, S. J.

First Reading
1 Corinthians 12:12-26 (Analogy of the body)

> *Silence*

Second Reading
Ephesians 4:1-16 (Unity of the body)

> *Pause*

Song
"A Time for Building Bridges" from *I Will Not Forget You*, by Carey Landry

> *Silence*

Suggestion
Stand or sit in a circle and join hands for spontaneous prayer and the closing.

> *Spontaneous Prayer*

Closing
Divine Spirit, free us from our fears so that we may have
the courage to be truthful and faithful
even when it brings pain or loss,
the compassion to stand up for the poor, or the minority,
even when it brings peer disapproval
and the humility to respect and be open to another's point of view
especially when it differs from our own.
Amen.

TESTAMENT THREADS:

Gladness of Heart

Opening
With hearts full of gladness and joy, let us prepare for our prayer together.

> *Pause*

Song
"Happy Man" from *Calm Is the Night*, by the Monks of Weston Priory

Instruction
As you read the testament threads, very softly play "The Meadow" from *The God of Life*, by John Michael Talbot

Readings
Psalm 1:1:
Happy the man who follows not
   the counsel of the wicked
Nor walks in the way of sinners,
   nor sits in the company of the insolent,
But delights in the law of the LORD
   and meditates on his law day and night.

      Pause

Psalm 1:3:
He is like a tree
   planted near running water,
That yields its fruit in due season,
   and whose leaves never fade.
   [Whatever he does, prospers.]

      Pause

Psalm 3:5:
When I call out to the LORD,
   he answers me from his holy mountain.

      Pause

Psalm 4:3b:
Why do you love what is vain and seek after falsehood?

      Pause

Psalm 4:4a:
Know that the LORD does wonders for his faithful one....

      Pause

Psalm 4:9:
As soon as I lie down, I fall peacefully asleep,
   for you alone, O LORD,

bring security to my dwelling.

Pause

Psalm 4:8:
You put gladness into my heart,
   more than when grain and wine abound.

Pause

Psalm 8:2:
O LORD, our Lord,
   how glorious is your name over all the earth!

Pause

Psalm 16:8:
I set the LORD ever before me;
   with him at my right hand I shall not be disturbed.

Pause

Song of Songs 2:8:
Hark! my lover—here he comes
   springing across the mountains,
   leaping across the hills.

Pause

Song of Songs 3:1:
On my bed at night I sought him
   whom my heart loves—
I sought him but I did not find him.

Pause

Song of Songs 3:2-4a:
I will rise then and go about the city;
   in the streets and crossings I will seek
Him whom my heart loves.
   I sought him but I did not find him.
The watchmen came upon me,
   as they made their rounds of the city:
   Have you seen him whom my heart loves?
I had hardly left them
   when I found him whom my heart loves.

Silence

Spontaneous Prayer

Song

"Father, Make Me Holy" from *The God of Life*, by John Michael Talbot

Closing

With glad hearts and praise for your name, Lord, we close our prayer. Amen.

SCRIPTURE THEME:

Calming the Waters

Opening

We open our prayer, calling on the name of Jesus who calms all of our fears. Let us invite him now to calm our hearts, our minds and our spirits.

Song

"Calm Is the Night" from *Calm Is the Night*, by the the Monks of Weston Priory

First Reading

Luke 8:22-25 (Jesus calms the storm.)

> *Pause*

Second Reading

Psalm 107:23-32 (God stills the storm.)

> *Pause*

Commentary

The boat people, telling about their dangerous journeys to our shores, say that the presence of one calm personality sometimes saved a whole boatload of passengers. Just one individual exhibiting faith and courage would inspire his or her fellow travelers to ride out the storm without giving in to panic.

> *Pause*

Christ is that calming influence in our lives. If we reflect *his* light, we can bring calm to others.

> *Pause*

Christ calms the storms of temptation.

> *Pause*

Christ calms the storms of passion.

> *Pause*

Christ calms the storms of sorrow.

> *Pause*

Christ calms the storms of fear.

Song
"Peace Is Flowing Like a River" from *I Will Not Forget You*, by Carey Landry

> *Silence*

> *Spontaneous Prayer*

Closing
As we close our prayer, let us remember that walking with Christ helps us conquer the storm. Amen.

MEDITATION THEME:

Personal Power

Opening
Free us, Father, so that we may connect with you, the higher power.

Song
"For We Are Free" from *Calm Is the Night*, by the Monks of Weston Priory

First Reading
John 8:31-36 (The truth will set you free.)

> *Pause*

Second Reading
John 14:12-14 (Believers will do Christ's works.)

Pause

Meditation Exercise
No one has the power to make you feel angry, fearful, sad, nervous. No one can alter your emotions unless you give someone that power. Usually, someone has that kind of hold over you and can manipulate or use you when that person has something you want (money, love, connections, etc.). If you are in such a situation, let go of whatever desire binds you to your oppressor. You may think this is a hard demand, but it isn't. Believe me, it is easier to give up that desire than to suffer the emotional bondage which wanting it brings. Trust, instead, that God will meet your needs. Really, your only need should be your relationship with God.

If you are having an upsetting day, call on God's higher power to free you from earthly desires and put joy in your heart. If *you* don't make your day joyful, who will? Blame no one but yourself. You have the power to be as happy as you decide you want to be.

Close your eyes now. Ask the Lord to flood you with rays of light and happiness. Bask in that happiness. Know that it is yours whenever you choose to reach for it. Rest in your joy. Rest in your happiness.

Silence

Song
"Fill My Cup, Lord" from *Cry Hosanna*, by Fisherfolk

Silence

Spontaneous Prayer

Closing
We close with this prayer:

May the power of the Holy Spirit
establish harmony and peace in our being.
Amen.

Counting the Cost

Song

"Holy God of Truth" from *The God of Life,* by John Michael Talbot

Opening

The theme of this prayer is counting the cost of discipleship. You will each have the opportunity to share aloud what the Scripture reading meant to you, so please listen attentively and allow the Scripture to speak to you personally.

>	*Pause*

Lord, free us from our thoughts and our worldly attachments so that we may open ourselves up to your Word.

>	*Pause*

First Reading

Luke 14:25-33 (Counting the cost)

>	*Silence*

Instructions

Each person may now share aloud what the Scripture meant to him or her. The sharing is intended to be a reflection of personal experience, not a sermon for others. Keep comments short—just a few sentences. This sharing should not turn into discussion. Be at ease with the silent gaps between comments.

>	*Sharing*

The same passage will be read aloud again. As you listen to it this time, reflect on the comments each person shared with the group.

Second Reading

Luke 14:25-33

Instructions

There will be a period of silence and then spontaneous prayer. The prayers spoken aloud should relate to the reading and its effect on you. For example, "God, give me the wisdom to serve you wisely and faithfully," or, "Lord, help me to serve you on your terms, not mine, and give me the grace to see clearly and accept those terms before I begin."

> *Silence*

> *Spontaneous Prayer*

Song
"Lose Yourself in Me" from *I Will Not Forget You*, by Carey Landry

Sharing Aids
If needed, the following questions may spark more sharing and can be used by the leader during the first round of sharing.

1) What does the word *renounce* mean when we speak of it in terms of family, friends, possessions?

2) What can we do to anticipate the "cost" of a project (a relationship, etc.) before making a commitment?

cycle 8

SCRIPTURE THEME:

Putting Your Hand to the Plow

Opening

Help us, Lord, to live fully in the moment without thought to guilt, worries or past injuries. Your kingdom is forgiveness and each day is a fresh beginning.

Song

"Like a Shepherd" from *A Dwelling Place*, by the St. Louis Jesuits

First Reading

Luke 9:57-62 (Putting your hand to the plow)

> *Pause*

Second Reading

From *St. Catherine of Siena*, by Johannes Jorgensen:

> "No man putting his hand to the plough and looking back is fit for the kingdom of God." That saying made a deep impression upon Catherine as did this one, "Let the dead bury their dead." It is a judgment upon all sentimentalism, upon all morbid brooding over the past, over a longing for a time that is gone, which was a time of sin and sorrow but which one loves because it is his own. Not to linger among the dead, not to long for the world of shadows, not to look back, but bravely to put one's hand to the plough and guide its iron-sheathed edge on through the golden-brown soil in the morning sun, under the dewy wet foliage of the olive trees—that was Catherine's ideal, her duty, her life.
>
> *Pause*

Song

"I Lift Up My Soul" from *A Dwelling Place*, by the St. Louis Jesuits

Silence

Spontaneous Prayer

Closing

As we close our prayer together, we lift up our souls to you, Yahweh. Amen.

PSALM THEME:

Forgiveness

Opening

Let us open our prayer by asking our Father to forgive us our trespasses as we forgive those who trespass against us.

Song

"Your Love is Changing the World" from *Cry Hosanna*, by Fisherfolk

Reading

Psalm 32 (Remission of sins)

Silence

Psalm 51 (Prayer of repentance)

Silence

Psalm 130 (Prayer for pardon and mercy)

Song

"Healer of My Soul" from *The God of Life*, by John Michael Talbot

Silence

Instructions

During the silent time, think of the people you have offended. Ask their forgiveness, and picture in your mind that they do forgive you and welcome you back into their hearts and lives. Then think of all those who have offended you and forgive each one's offense. In your minds, picture yourself embracing each of them.

Sometimes it is hard to do this but remember what Jesus has told us: "Pardon and you shall be pardoned" (Luke 6:36b).

This can be an emotional experience for some. Be sure to comfort one another through prayer and touch. Spontaneous prayers may be spoken or silent. Each person should feel free to move with the Spirit of forgiveness working within.

> *Spontaneous Prayer*

Closing
We close our prayer, thanking you for your mercy and compassion, Lord.

Laborers in the Vineyard

Opening
Let us begin in the name of the Lord.

Song
"Fill My Cup, Lord" from *Cry Hosanna*, by Fisherfolk

First Reading
Matthew 20:1-16 (Laborers in the vineyard)

> *Pause*

Second Reading
From "A Storyteller's Story of Prayer," an interview with John Shea in *Praying*:

> The story suggests that at the core of our makeup there is a chronic envy and resentment. And we live out of that. As a result, we judge ourselves only in relationship with other people, usually the people who have what we really want. We always judge ourselves in envious and resentful ways. The workers feel cheated because their only way of evaluating themselves is in comparison to the good fortune of others.
>
> When you get inside the parable of the vineyard

and meditate on it, then you begin to focus on your own life. How does resentment work with you? How does envy work with you? Some people are in such a chronic state of envy that they don't even know it anymore.

The story really works in this way because it gets everybody ticked off. People hate the story. I have never told it where people liked it. And they all try to rationalize it. One common rationalization is that the men who worked only an hour worked real hard. No, that ain't it. The question is: Why do you respond to the story by getting mad? Then you have to go back and look at the reason.

Ask yourself. Why are you mad? What would you do if you were one of the workers who worked all day? You hear the story and you are judged but also you are hopeful because you know that something is working within you. You are hopeful that maybe there is a new way and that you don't have to live in this type of resentment. In the middle class parish where I work, resentment and envy are two of the most self-destructive vices of the neighborhood. Men live in resentment because of promotions or lack of them, money or lack of it and the injustices that they experience.

The parable also has another meaning for me. You only know who you are when you know who somebody else isn't. You only know you are somebody when someone else gets less pay. As a result, you have a vested envy when they get ahead of you.

Silence

Song
"Betwixt Me and My Brother" from *The God of Life*, by John Michael Talbot

Silence

Spontaneous Prayer

Closing
We thank you, Father, for hearing our prayers—both those we have spoken and the silent, unspoken prayers of our hearts.

MEDITATION THEME:

Seizing the Kingdom by Force

Opening
Let us open our prayer with a minute of silence.

Song
"No Longer Strangers" from *No Longer Strangers*, by John Michael Talbot

Scripture Reading
Matthew 11:7-15 (Taking the kingdom by force)

Pause

Commentary
John the Baptist was the greatest born among men because of the talent and gifts bestowed on him from on high. However, none of this matters as much as a contrite heart turned toward the Kingdom of God.

The violent who have been seizing heaven by force are those Christians who fight for the kingdom through prayer, fasting, divine reading and reaching out, unselfishly, to others.

John's example was not one of passive Christian waiting for heaven, but of an active creative personality searching and striving to serve the kingdom wherever he found himself—in the solitude of the desert praying, among the crowds of the city preaching or in the depths of a dungeon preparing for death.

Pause

Talented and gifted people do not necessarily inherit the kingdom as quickly as their lesser brothers and sisters who are actively engaged in building a kingdom of love right here, rather than acquiring prestige and possessions for themselves.

Pause

Meditation Exercise
Close your eyes and picture Jesus walking toward you. From a long way off he is moving toward you slowly. He is radiant with joy because *you* are one of his creations and he is going to tell you about your gifts and how you can use them in his service. What does he say to you?

Silence

Song
"The Servant Song" from *Cry Hosanna,* by Fisherfolk

Silence

Suggestion
Let your spontaneous prayers echo your meditation (i.e., "Lord, give me the courage to place my gifts at your feet").

Spontaneous Prayer

Closing
We close our prayer in the name of God, our creator. Amen.

SCRIPTURE THEME:

Trust in God, Not Riches

Opening
As we join together for prayer, teach us, Lord, to be responsible stewards.

Song
Isaiah 58 from *No Longer Strangers,* by John Michael Talbot

First Reading
Luke 16:19-31 (The rich man and Lazarus)

Pause

Questions to Ponder
How does our culture influence us and lead us into serving the god of money rather than the God of creation?

In our society, why can one man pay thousands of dollars for an artificial organ to increase his life span a year or so while elsewhere a child starves for lack of food?

Is participation in high-interest notes a structure that adds to the oppression of the poor?

Second Reading
Psalm 49 (The vanity of riches)

Song

"Trust in the Lord" from *A Dwelling Place*, by the St. Louis Jesuits

Silence

Spontaneous Prayer

Closing

May this prayer be extended into our workaday lives and allow us to trust in God's wisdom. Amen.

TESTAMENT THREADS:

Peace

Opening

Let us begin in the name of the Prince of Peace.

Song

"Peace Prayer" from *A Dwelling Place*, by the St. Louis Jesuits

Readings

Ezekiel 36:26a:

I will give you a new heart and place a new spirit within you....

Pause

Ezekiel 36:27:

I will put my Spirit with you and make you live by my statutes, careful to observe my decrees.

Pause

Isaiah 54:10:

Though the mountains leave their place
    and the hills be shaken,
My love shall never leave you
    nor my covenant of peace be shaken
    says the LORD, who has mercy on you.

Pause

Psalm 72:3

The mountains shall yield peace for the people,
    and the hills justice.

Pause

Matthew 5:9:
Blest are the peacemakers,
they shall be called sons [and daughters] of God.

Pause

Thomas à Kempis:
All men desire peace but few desire the things that make for peace.

Pause

Pilgrims' Way:
Peace is that state in which fear of any kind is unknown.

Pause

Thomas Wilson:
The fewer desires, the more peace.

Pause

Luke 2:14:
"Glory to God in high heaven,
   peace on earth to those on whom his favor rests."

Song
"Peace Is Flowing Like a River" from *I Will Not Forget You*, by
Carey Landry

Suggestion
During the silent time, think of the recent occasions when you
have not been at peace. How often has greed been at the bottom
of your lack of peace? Are you trying to cram too much activity
or work into too short a time? Are you working hard to provide
yourself and your family with luxuries? Are you anxious about
relationships because you want others to live up to your
expectations? Remember Thomas Wilson's remark, "The fewer
desires, the more peace."

Silence

Spontaneous Prayer

Closing
Share a sign of peace (handshake, hug, kiss) with each other. Then
join hands and sing the Great Amen.

Following Jesus

Opening

Let us begin our prayer in the name of Jesus.

First Reading

From *Following Jesus*, by Segundo Galilea:

> Following Jesus in his love for his brothers and sisters and for the poor, even being ready to give our lives, is not the result of our own strength or our own will. To be faithful to this following—not just for a time or under an impulse of youth or enthusiasm, but rather for our entire lives—goes beyond our possibilities. But what is impossible for humans is possible for God. What turns us from egoists to followers is to encounter the presence of Christ in our lives both through contemplative prayer and through service. Through prayer we receive the same gift that Christ offered to the Samaritan woman at Jacob's well—a kind of inexhaustible water which will never allow us to thirst.

Song

"Fill My Cup, Lord" from *Cry Hosanna*, by Fisherfolk

Second Reading

John 4:7-15 (Woman at the well)

> *Pause*

Third Reading

From *Following Jesus*, by Segundo Galilea:

> Through service we also encounter the person of Christ by the experience of the presence of Christ in our brothers and sisters.

> *Pause*

Fourth Reading

Matthew 25:31-46 (The last judgment)

Song

"Brother Jesus" from *I Will Not Forget You*, by Carey Landry

> *Silence*

> *Spontaneous Prayer*

Closing
We close our prayer in the name of Jesus.

Silence

Opening
Let us begin by taking a few minutes of silence to set aside our worldly cares and find God in the stillness of our hearts.

Song
"Lose Yourself in Me" from *I Will Not Forget You*, by Carey Landry

First Reading
Psalm 131 (A quieted heart)

> *Pause*

Meditation Exercise
Silence is the golden road to communion with the divine. True silence involves the setting aside of self to make room for God. The hardest thing in the world is to tame one's thoughts but, with practice, it can be done. The fruits of this exercise are peace and calm and a knowledge which passes all understanding.

Close your eyes now and concentrate on any color you wish. If you have difficulty concentrating: Pretend you are looking at the sky and picture the color blue. Or pretend you are looking at the moon and picture the color white. Or imagine a field of green grass and picture the color green.

As thoughts distract you, keep returning to your color. You will be surprised at the results.

Song
"Peace to You" from *Calm Is the Night*, by the Monks of Weston Priory

> *Silence*

Spontaneous Prayer

Closing
Our prayer together is ended. Let us go forth in peace.

Celebrate Life

Song
"Alleluia, He Is Coming" from *Cry Hosanna,* by Fisherfolk

Opening
The theme of this prayer is the celebration of life. You will each have the opportunity to share aloud what the Scripture reading meant to you, so please listen attentively and allow the Scripture to speak to you personally.

Pause

Speak to us, Lord. Help us listen to your Word and to enjoy being silent in one another's presence.

Pause

First Reading
Matthew 9:14-18 (Celebrate while the bridegroom is with you.)

Silence

Instructions
Each person may now share aloud what the Scripture meant to him or her. The sharing is intended to be a reflection of personal experience, not a sermon for others. Keep comments short—just a few sentences. This sharing should not turn into discussion. Be at ease with the silent gaps between comments.

Sharing

The same passage will be read aloud again. As you listen to it this time, reflect on the comments each person shared with the group.

Second Reading
Matthew 9:14-18

Instructions

There will be a period of silence and then spontaneous prayer. The prayers spoken aloud should relate to the reading and its effect on you. For example, "Lord, help me to understand you in a new way," or, "Teach me, Jesus, the joys of celebrating with you."

> *Silence*

> *Spontaneous Prayer*

Song

"Fill My Cup, Lord" from *Cry Hosanna,* by Fisherfolk

Sharing Aids

If needed, the following questions may spark more sharing and can be used by the leader during the first round of sharing.

1) When Christ is with us, it is a time of celebration. When Christ is not with us, it is a time of fasting. If we brought Christ into our life more often, could we then celebrate more often?

2) Christ is telling us not to treat new cloth like old cloth or new wine like old wine. The new cannot be treated like the old. What does this mean? "The new" what? "The old" what?

cycle 9

SCRIPTURE THEME:

The Simple Life

Opening

We open our prayer, Lord, seeking the simplicity necessary to be constantly aware that it is in you that we live and move and have our being.

Song

"Flowers Still Grow There" from *Wood Hath Hope*, by John Foley, S. J.

First Reading

1 Timothy 6:6-10 (Be content with sufficiency.)

Pause

Second Reading

From *The Song of the Bird*, by Anthony de Mello, S. J.:

> The rich industrialist from the North was horrified to find the Southern fisherman lying lazily beside his boat, smoking a pipe.
>
> "Why aren't you out fishing?" said the industrialist.
>
> "Because I have caught enough fish for the day," said the fisherman.
>
> "Why don't you catch more than you need?" said the industrialist.
>
> "What would I do with it?" asked the fisherman.
>
> "You could earn more money," was the reply. "With that you could have a motor fixed to your boat. Then you could go into deeper waters and catch more fish. Then you would make enough to buy nets. These would bring you more fish and more money. Soon you would

have enough money to own two boats—maybe even a fleet of boats. Then you would be rich like me."

"What would I do then?" asked the fisherman.

"Then you could sit down and enjoy life," said the industrialist.

"What do you think I am doing right now?" said the contented fisherman.

Pause

Third Reading
Psalm 131 (A humble and quiet heart)

Song
"Peace Is Flowing Like a River" from *I Will Not Forget You*, by Carey Landry

Silence

Spontaneous prayer

Closing
Our prayer is ended. Let us go in peace to serve the Lord and one another.

PSALM THEME:

Guidance

Opening
As we begin our prayer, we lift up our souls to you, Yahweh.

Song
"I Lift Up My Soul" from *A Dwelling Place*, by the St. Louis Jesuits

Readings
Psalm 25 (Prayer for guidance and help)

Silence

Psalm 40 (Delight in God's will)

Silence

Psalm 119:1-8 (Praise of God's law)

Pause

Psalm 119:17-20 (Desire for God's law)

Pause

Psalm 119:33-40 (Prayer for guidance)

Pause

Psalm 119:73-77 (The justice of God's law)

Pause

Psalm 119:129-136 (Love for God's law)

Song
"Nature and Grace" from *No Longer Strangers,* by John Michael Talbot

Suggestion
These psalm readings should open you to God's will. Now reach out to one another by gathering in a circle (on the floor or around a table) and holding hands during the period of silence and the spontaneous prayer. Your petitions might be especially directed to building community, meeting each other's needs, etc.

Silence

Spontaneous Prayer

Closing
Our prayer together is ended. Let us go forth to do God's will.

SCRIPTURE THEME:

The Way, the Truth and the Light

Opening
We begin our prayer in the name of our brother, Jesus.

Song
"Brother Jesus" from *I Will Not Forget You,* by Carey Landry

First Reading
John 14:1-6 (The way, the truth, the light)

Pause

Second Reading
Psalm 25:1-15 (Prayer for guidance)

Song
"Holy God of Truth" from *The God of Life*, by John Michael Talbot

Pause

Suggestion
Each one of you is a unique, beautiful creation that will not be duplicated throughout the eons of the universe. Imagine your originality! And God relates to each one of you in a special, personal way—every path is as unique as the individual.

During the silent time, meditate on the "way" Jesus is leading you. In what way are you following and in what way are you resisting?

Silence

Spontaneous Prayer

Closing
We thank you, Lord, for hearing our prayers and showing us the way. Amen.

MEDITATION THEME:

Thanksgiving

Opening
We open our prayer with hearts full of gratitude and praise. Let us pause to give thanks for the beauty of creation which surrounds us.

Pause

Song
"Thanks to Thee" from *The God of Life*, by John Michael Talbot

Pause

Scripture Reading
Luke 17:11-19 (Ten lepers)

Pause

Meditation Exercise

Ask the Lord why he has favored you in such a way that your home is filled with gadgets, conveniences and luxuries while others have no roofs over their heads. Listen carefully to his answer and meditate on what that means in your life.

Silence

Song

"Servant Song" from *Cry Hosanna*, by Fisherfolk

Silence

Spontaneous Prayer

Suggestions

Invite participants to share something from their meditation experiences if they wish.

Closing

We close our prayer in thanksgiving for your love and divine benevolence. Amen.

SCRIPTURE THEME:

Watchfulness

Opening

Let us open our prayer with watchful hearts as we wait upon the Lord.

Pause

Song

"Calm Is the Night" from *Calm Is the Night*, by the Monks of Weston Priory

First Reading

Matthew 25:1-13 (The ten virgins)

Pause

Second Reading
Mark 13:32-37 (Watchfulness)

Pause

Suggestion
After the following song and during the quiet time, practice waiting
on the Lord by focusing on a color as you did in the meditation
exercise on p. 108. Putting our needs aside and focusing in silence
is a wonderful discipline for watchfulness. If you have trouble
concentrating, pretend you are looking at the sky and see the color
blue. Or pretend you are looking at the moon and see the color
white. Or imagine a field of grass and see the color green.

Song
"We Go On Waiting" from *Calm Is the Night,* by the Monks of
Weston Priory

Silence

Spontaneous Prayer

Closing
Keep our spirits watchful, God, as we go forth from our prayer
together. Amen.

TESTAMENT THREADS:

Faith

Opening
In the Spirit of faith, we open our prayer.

Song
"Isaiah 49" from *I Will Not Forget You,* by Carey Landry

Readings
Mark 4:35-40:
That day as evening drew on he said to them, "Let us cross over
to the farther shore." Leaving the crowd, they took him away in
the boat in which he was sitting, while the other boats
accompanied him. It happened that a bad squall blew up. The
waves were breaking over the boat and it began to ship water

badly. Jesus was in the stern through it all, sound asleep on a cushion. They finally woke him and said to him, "Teacher, does it not matter to you that we are going to drown?" And he awoke and rebuked the wind, and said to the sea, "Quiet! Be still!" The wind fell off and everything grew calm. Then he said to them, "Why are you so terrified? Why are you lacking in faith?"

Pause

Mark 5:25-34:
There was a woman in the area who had been afflicted with a hemorrhage for a dozen years. She had received treatment at the hands of doctors of every sort and exhausted her savings in the process, yet she got no relief; on the contrary, she only grew worse. She had heard about Jesus and came up behind him in the crowd and put her hand to his cloak. "If I just touch his clothing," she thought, "I shall get well." Immediately her flow of blood dried up and the feeling that she was cured of her affliction ran through her whole body. Jesus was conscious at once that healing power had gone out from him. Wheeling about in the crowd, he began to ask, "Who touched my clothing?" His disciples said to him, "You can see how this crowd hems you in, yet you ask, 'Who touched me?'" Despite this, he kept looking around to see the woman who had done it. Fearful and beginning to tremble now as she realized what had happened, the woman came and fell in front of him and told him the whole truth. He said to her, "Daughter, it is your faith that has cured you. Go in peace and be free of this illness."

Silence

Mark 11:20-23:
Early next moring, as they were walking along, they saw the fig tree withered away to its roots. Peter remembered and said to him, "Rabbi, look! The fig tree you cursed has withered up." In reply Jesus told them, "Put your trust in God. I solemnly assure you, whoever says to this mountain, 'Be lifted up and thrown into the sea,' and has no inner doubts, believes that what he says will happen, shall have it done for him. I give you my word, if you are ready to believe that you will receive whatever you ask for in prayer, it shall be done for you."

Pause

Matthew 17:14-18:
As they approached the crowd, a man came up to him and knelt before him. "Lord," he said, "take pity on my son, who is demented and in a serious condition. For example, he often falls into the fire and frequently into the water. I have brought him to your disciples but they could not cure him." In reply Jesus said: "What an unbelieving and perverse lot you are! How long must I remain with you? How long can I endure you? Bring him here to me!" Then Jesus reprimanded him, and the demon came out of him. That very moment the boy was cured.

Pause

Matthew 17:19-21:
The disciples approached Jesus at that point and asked him privately, "Why could we not expel it?" "Because you have so little trust," he told them. "I assure you, if you had faith the size of a mustard seed, you would be able to say to this mountain, 'Move from here to there,' and it would move. Nothing would be impossible for you. [This kind does not leave but by prayer and fasting.]"

Song
"Brother Jesus" from *I Will Not Forget You,* by Carey Landry

Silence

Spontaneous Prayer

Closing
In the name of Jesus, we close our prayer. Amen.

SCRIPTURE THEME:

Weaknesses

Opening
Our prayer theme is weaknesses. Let us begin our prayer by taking a moment to get in touch with our shadows—those areas which we prefer to leave in the dark.

Pause

Song
"Nature and Grace" from *No Longer Strangers*, by John Michael Talbot

First Reading
1 Corinthians 1:26—2:5 (The status of the Corinthians)

Pause

Commentary
If God chose what was low and despised in this world, why are we afraid to look at those parts of ourselves that we despise? Instead of being afraid, we should reach out to those dark areas and treat them as lost sheep, welcoming them back to the fold. This is the way to wholeness—that is, to holiness. Completeness is not perfection but recognition of our entire self—both the light and dark sides of our nature. And as we become more gentle, more accepting of our own weaknesses, we become more gentle and accepting of others' weaknesses.

Pause

Second Reading
2 Corinthians 12:1-10 (Thorn in Paul's flesh)

Pause

Song
"Healer of My Soul" from *The God of Life*, by John Michael Talbot

Silence

Suggestion
Let your prayer reflect the theme. Pray out loud or in silence for acceptance and redemption of at least one weakness.

Spontaneous Prayer

Closing
During this prayer session we have embraced our weaknesses with love and forgiveness. Now let us embrace one another in the same spirit.

Bicycling With God

Opening
Let us prepare for this prayer by entering into a spirit of surrender.

Song
"Lose Yourself in Me" from *I Will Not Forget You*, by Carey Landry

First Reading
John 12:24-26 (The grain of wheat)

>*Pause*

Second Reading
Matthew 10:39 (Self-discovery)

Third Reading
"Bicycling With God," (author unknown):

>At first I saw God as my observer, my judge, keeping track of the things I did wrong, so as to know whether I merited heaven or hell when I die. He was out there sort of like the president. I recognized his picture when I saw it, but I didn't really know him.
>
>But later on when I recognized my higher power, it seemed as though life was rather like a bike ride, but it was a tandem bike, and I noticed that God was in the back helping me pedal.
>
>I don't know just when it was that he suggested we change places, but life has not been the same since, life with my higher power, that is. God makes life exciting!
>
>When I had control, I knew the way. It was rather boring but predictable. It was the shortest distance between two points.
>
>But when he took the lead, he knew delightful long cuts, up mountains, and through rocky places and at breakneck speeds; it was all I could do to hang on! Even though it looked like madness, he said, "Pedal."
>
>I worried and was anxious and asked, "Where are you taking me?" He laughed and didn't answer and I started to learn to trust.

I forgot my boring life and entered into the adventure. And when I'd say, "I'm scared," he'd lean back and touch my hand.

He took me to people with gifts that I needed, gifts of healing, acceptance and joy. They gave me their gifts to take on my journey, our journey, God's and mine.

And we were off again. He said, "Give the gifts away; they're extra baggage, too much weight." So I did, to the people we met, and I found that in giving I received and still our burden was light.

I did not trust him at first, in control of my life. I thought he'd wreck it. But he knows bike secrets, knows how to make it bend to take sharp corners, jump to clear high rocks, fly to shorten scary passages.

And I am learning to shut up and pedal in the strangest places, and I'm beginning to enjoy the view and the cool breeze on my face with my delightful constant companion, my higher power.

And when I'm sure I just can't do any more, he just smiles and says, "Pedal."

Pause

Meditation Exercise

Meditate on those areas in your life where you are hanging onto the controls. You'll know these areas because they are the concerns which bring anxiety, loss of sleep, worry, etc.

Pause

What do you fear if you let go of the controls?

Pause

Can you let go, prayerfully, if you know you are turning the controls over to God?

Pause

How can you begin to turn over the controls to God? Meditate on this in silence.

Silence

Song
"The Lord's Prayer" from *Calm Is the Night*, by the Monks of Weston Priory

Closing
Join hands and say the Lord's Prayer together.

COLLATIO:

The Prodigal Son

Song
"Isaiah 49" from *I Will Not Forget You*, by Carey Landry

Opening
The theme of this prayer is the Prodigal Son. You will each have the opportunity to share aloud what the Scripture reading meant to you, so please listen attentively and allow the Scripture to speak to you personally.

> *Pause*

Speak to us, Lord. Help us listen to your Word and to enjoy being silent in each other's presence.

> *Pause*

First Reading
Luke 15:11-32 (The Prodigal Son)

> *Silence*

Instructions
Each person may now share aloud what the Scripture meant to her or him. The sharing is intended to be a reflection of personal experience, not a sermon for others. Keep comments short—just a few sentences. This sharing should not turn into discussion. Be at ease with the silent gaps between comments.

> *Sharing*

The same passage will be read aloud again. As you listen to it this time, reflect on the comments each person shared with the group.

Second Reading
Luke 15:11-32

Instructions
There will be a period of silence and then spontaneous prayer.
The prayers spoken aloud should relate to the reading and its
effect on you. For example, "Father, give me the humility always
to return to you," or, "Father, thank you for loving me no matter
how far I stray from home."

Silence

Spontaneous Prayer

Closing Song
"Holy God of Truth" from *The God of Life*, by John Michael Talbot

Sharing Aids
If needed, the following questions may spark more sharing and
can be used by the leader during the first round of sharing.

1) With whom did you identify in the story? Were you the
father, the older brother or the prodigal son?

2) Many people identify with the older brother. If you
identified with him, ask yourself why and get in touch with the
emotions that were sparked in you as you heard the story.

3) Do you have a feeling that in this story (and in other Gospel
stories) the sinner gets off easy? That the boy has fun all his life
then gets back in the father's graces at the last minute while the
faithful one gets treated unfairly? If your answer is yes, try to
unmask the conditioning that makes you feel this way.

4) Do you think the sinner is really having fun and that the
righteous person lives a drab, boring life? Or does the person who
is striving to live and build the kingdom here on earth already
have a reward in happiness and a sense of fulfillment?

cycle 10

Risk

Opening
Spirit of Life, grant us the daring to seek out our Creator
adventurously.

Song
"Trust in the Lord" from *A Dwelling Place*, by the St. Louis Jesuits

First Reading
1 John 3:11-24 (Loving one another)

Pause

Commentary
For those on the spiritual journey, there is a strong temptation to
put up a tent and stay within its safety rather than risk the hazards
of life on the open road. Mature sojourners, however, must come
out of their comfortable, spiritual covers and enter into the agony
and ecstasy of the drama of life. This involves the courage to aid
fellow travelers on the road, especially those who have broken
down along the way.

Pause

Second Reading
John 13:33-35 ("Love one another.")

Song
"One Bread, One Body" from *Wood Hath Hope*, by John Foley, S. J.

Silence

Spontaneous Prayer

Closing

We close our prayer recognizing that we are all sisters and brothers traveling on the road to our Father's house. Amen.

Prayers for Help

Opening

Let us begin our prayer in the name of the Lord.

Song

"Our Help Is From the Lord" from *Wood Hath Hope*, by John Foley, S. J.

Reading

Psalm 86 (Prayer in distress)

> *Silence*

Psalm 13 (Prayer in sorrow)

> *Pause*

Song

"Isaiah 49" from *I Will Not Forget You*, by Carey Landry

> *Silence*

> *Spontaneous Prayer*

Closing

We close our prayer, Lord, with hearts grateful for your eternal love.

Awareness and Peace

Opening

We open our prayer in the name of the Prince of Peace.

Song

"Peace Prayer" from *A Dwelling Place*, by the St. Louis Jesuits

First Reading

Matthew 5:38-46 (Love of enemies)

> *Pause*

Second Reading

From "Awareness and Peace," by Thicth Nhat Hanh (*Catholic Worker Newsletter*):

> Our daily life has much to do with government. I want to talk to you about the way people in Japan drank tea in the past. It took them three hours to drink a cup of tea. You would say that this is very much a waste of time because time is money. But two people being with each other and spending three hours drinking tea, I think that has something to do with peace. Please do not imagine that the two men or two women speak a lot to each other. No, they don't speak much. They exchange only one word or two, but they are there. They enjoy the three hours and a few cups of tea. They know really what the tea is and they know really what the presence of each other means to them.
>
> Nowadays we only have a few minutes for a cup of tea. We go into a cafe and we order a cup of tea and we listen to all kinds of music and we listen to a lot of noises and we think of the business we are going to do after the tea. So the tea does not really exist and we do violence to the tea.
>
> Pick up a newspaper to read in the morning, say the *New York Times*. I have seen and I have touched the Sunday edition of the *New York Times*. It is so heavy I believe to make such an edition they would have to cut down a whole forest. And the *New York Times* is not the only newspaper in this country. There are several like that and we are destroying our earth without knowing it if we pick up our daily papers without being aware of what we are doing.
>
> So, drinking a cup of tea or picking up a newspaper has to do with peace. Nonviolence has another name, awareness. We should be aware of what we are, of who

we are and of what we are doing.

Silence

Third Reading
Isaiah 11:6-9 (The lion and the lamb)

Pause

Song
"Peace Is Flowing Like a River" from *I Will Not Forget You,* by Carey Landry

Suggestion
Gather around in a circle, on the floor or around a table, with a candle in the center. Hold hands in silence for several minutes. As the Spirit moves each, some may pray aloud, some may remain silent.

Silence

Spontaneous Prayer

Closing
Still holding hands, say the Our Father together.

SCRIPTURE THEME:

Mercy

Opening
Let us begin our prayer in the name of the God of mercy.

Song
"Blest Be the Lord" from *A Dwelling Place,* by the St. Louis Jesuits

First Reading
1 Timothy 1:12-17 (Christ deals with us mercifully.)

Pause

Second Reading
Psalm 145:8-21 (The Lord's mercy)

Pause

Suggestion

During the silent time, meditate on divine mercy. Picture Jesus looking down at you from the cross. He forgave his executioners; he will have mercy on you too if you only ask for it. In a sense it was easier for Christ to forgive his executioners than to forgive his disciples. The Roman soldiers "did not know what they were doing." But what about the apostles who had been with him for years and were continually refreshed by his love and his wisdom? What kind of support did any of them (except John) offer Jesus during his crucifixion? Yet Christ was merciful to them because he understood their fears and weaknesses just as he understands ours.

Silence

Song

"Alleluia, He Is Coming" from *Cry Hosanna*, by Fisherfolk

Silence

Spontaneous Prayer

Closing

We close our prayer in thanksgiving for God's mercy. Amen.

SCRIPTURE THEME:

Detachment

Opening

Our theme is detachment. Let us begin our prayer in the name of God.

Song

"Lose Yourself in Me" from *I Will Not Forget You*, by Carey Landry

First Reading

Luke 9:57-62 (Detachment)

Pause

Second Reading

From *Breakthrough*, by Matthew Fox:

> "A detached man," Meister Eckhart says, "experiences such a joy that no one would be able to tear it away from him. But such a man remains unsettled. He who has let himself be and who has let God be, lives in wandering joy, or joy without a cause.
>
> "Attachment to prayer, to fasting, to vigils, to all kinds of exterior exercises and mortifications, to any work or ministry, deprives us of the freedom to serve God in this present now."

> *Pause*

Third Reading

Philippians 4:10-13 (Paul's experience)

Fourth Reading

From *Breakthrough*:

> According to Meister Eckhart, "As long as in one way or another we seek our own advantage, we will never find God for we do not seek God exclusively. We must love God equally in all things. That is, love God as willingly in poverty as in riches and cherish him as much in sickness as in health, hold him as dear in temptation as without temptation, in suffering as much as without suffering."

Song

"For We Are Free" from *Calm Is the Night*, by the Monks of Weston Priory

> *Silence*

> *Spontaneous Prayer*

Closing

Our prayer is ended. Let us go forth to serve the Lord with joy and detachment.

'Ask and You Shall Receive'

Opening

"Here I stand, knocking at the door. If anyone hears me calling and opens the door, I will enter his house and have supper with him and he with me." (Revelation 3:20)

Song

"The Spirit Within Us" from *Calm Is the Night*, by the Monks of Weston Priory

Reading

Matthew 18:19-20:

"Again I tell you, if two of you join your voices on earth to pray for anything whatever, it shall be granted you by my Father in heaven. Where two or three are gathered in my name, there am I in their midst."

Pause

Luke 11:2a-4:

"Father,
hallowed be your name,
your kingdom come.
Give us each day our daily bread.
Forgive us our sins
for we too forgive all who do us wrong;
and subject us not to the trial."

Pause

Luke 11:9-13:

"So I say to you, 'Ask and you shall receive; seek and you shall find; knock and it shall be opened to you.'

"For whoever asks, receives; whoever seeks, finds; whoever knocks, is admitted. What father among you will give his son a snake if he asks for a fish, or hand him a scorpion if he asks for an egg? If you, with all your sins, know how to give your children good things, how much more will the heavenly Father give the Holy Spirit to those who ask him."

Silence

1 John 5:13-15:
I have written this to you to make you realize that you possess
eternal life—you who believe in the name of the Son of God.
    We have this confidence in God: that he hears us whenever
we ask for anything according to his will. And since we know that
he hears us whenever we ask, we know that what we have asked
him for is ours.

> *Pause*

Psalm 28:6-7:
Blessed be the LORD
    for he has heard the sound of my pleading;
    the LORD is my strength and my shield.
In him my heart trusts, and I find help;
    then my heart exults, and with my song I give him thanks.

> *Pause*

Song
"Dwelling Place" from *A Dwelling Place,* by the St. Louis Jesuits

> *Silence*

> *Spontaneous Prayer*

Closing
Join hands and say the Lord's Prayer.

SCRIPTURE THEME:

God Is Fire

Opening
We begin our prayer in the name of God, our creator.

Song
"God" from *The God of Life,* by John Michael Talbot

First Reading
Exodus 3:1-12 (The burning bush)

> *Pause*

Second Reading
1 Peter 4:12-19 (Trial by fire)

Third Reading
From *Zorba the Greek,* by Nikos Kazantzakis:

> "God is not cool water—no, he's not cool water to drink
> for refreshment. God is fire and you must walk upon
> it; not only walk but, most difficult of all, you must
> dance on this fire. And the moment you are able to
> dance on it, the fire will become cool water; but until
> you reach that point, what a struggle, my Lord, what
> agony."

> *Pause*

Song
"Behold the Wood" from *A Dwelling Place,* by the St. Louis Jesuits

> *Silence*

> *Spontaneous Prayers*

Closing
We close our prayer with a quote from the Gospel of Luke, "I have
come to light a fire on the earth. How I wish the blaze were
ignited!" (Luke 12:49).

MEDITATION THEME:

Servants

Opening
"Speak, LORD, for your servant is listening" (1 Samuel 3:9b).

Song
"Servant Song" from *Cry Hosanna,* by Fisherfolk

First Reading
John 13:1-17 (Washing of feet)

> *Pause*

Second Reading
Luke 22:24-27 (On authority)

Pause

Third Reading
Luke 17:7-10 ("Useless servants")

Pause

Fourth Reading
From *Jesus Before Christianity*, by Albert Nolan:

> The Kingdom of God, then, will be a society in which
> there will be no prestige and no status, no division of
> people into inferior and superior. Everyone will be
> loved and respected not because of his education or
> wealth or ancestry or authority or rank or virtue or
> other achievements, but because he, like everybody
> else, is a person. Some will find it very difficult to
> imagine what such a life would be like but the "babes"
> who have never had any of the privileges of status and
> those who have not valued it will find it very easy to
> appreciate the fulfillment that life in such a society
> would bring. Those who could not bear to have beggars,
> former prostitutes, servants, women and children
> treated as their equals, who could not live without
> feeling superior to at least some people, would simply
> not be at home in God's Kingdom as Jesus understood
> it. They would want to exclude themselves from it.
>
> The power of Satan is the power of domination
> and oppression, the power of God is the power of
> service and freedom. All the kingdoms and nations of
> this present world are governed by the power of
> domination of force. The structure of the Kingdom of
> God will be determined by the power of the
> spontaneous loving service which people render to one
> another.

Meditation Exercise
Think of God's Kingdom of love and service where everyone has
dignity. Immerse yourself in the possibility of this happening
around you—especially in your home and in your workplace. How
could your service to others help to bring it about? Ask the Lord
to show you the answer.

Silence

Song

"Betwixt Me and My Brother" from *The God of Life,* by John Michael Talbot

>*Pause*

>*Spontaneous Prayer*

Closing

Our prayer is ended. Let us go and serve one another. Amen.

COLLATIO:

'My Yoke Is Easy'

Song

"Flowers Still Grow There," from *Wood Hath Hope* by John Foley, S. J.

Opening

The theme of our prayer is the celebration of life. You will each have the opportunity to share aloud what the Scripture reading meant to you, so please listen attentively and allow the Scripture to speak to you personally.

>*Pause*

Speak to us, Lord. Help us listen to your Word and to enjoy being silent in each other's presence.

>*Pause*

First Reading

Matthew 11:28-30 ("Come to Me...")

>*Silence*

Instructions

Each person may now share aloud what the Scripture meant to him or her. The sharing is intended to be a reflection of personal experience, not a sermon for others. Keep comments short—just a few sentences. This sharing should not turn into discussion. Be at ease with the silent gaps between comments.

Sharing

The same passage will be read aloud again. As you listen to it this time, reflect on the comments each person shared with the group.

Second Reading
Matthew 11:28-30

Instructions
There will be a period of silence and then spontaneous prayer. The prayers spoken aloud should relate to the reading and its effect on you. For example, "Lord, help me to maintain a light, cheerful heart in all my relationships and responsibilities."

Silence

Spontaneous Prayer

Closing Song
"Fill My Cup, Lord" from *Cry Hosanna*, by Fisherfolk

Sharing Aids
If needed, the following questions may spark more sharing and can be used by the leader during the first round of sharing.

1) Do you agree with the statement that if your burden is overwhelming, it is a burden you have assumed for yourself and not the one God gave you?

2) Do we as Christians put too much emphasis on suffering and even suffer some things which we should have the courage and faith to change?

index

Other Resources for Small Groups

Relax and Pray! *Eight Guided Meditations.* By Virginia Froehle, R.S.M. CAS 180 $15.95

Relax and Hear! *Scriptural Meditations to Comfort and Challenge.* By Virginia Froehle, R.S.M. CAS 365 $16.95

In Her Presence: Prayer Experiences Exploring Feminine Images of God. By Virginia Froehle, R.S.M. CAS 440 $18.95

A Living-Room Retreat: *Meditations for Home Use, With a 12-Week Plan for Group Sharing.* By Helen Cecilia Swift, S.N.D. de N. SBN 954 $3.50

Taped Direction for the 12 Group Meetings of **A Living-Room Retreat.** By Helen Cecilia Swift, S.N.D. de N. CAS 020 $15.95

How Blest You Are! *A Living-Room Retreat Based on the Beatitudes.* By Helen Cecilia Swift, S.N.D. de N. SBN 330 $3.50

Taped Direction for the Nine Group Meetings of **How Blest You Are!** By Helen Cecilia Swift, S.N.D. de N. CAS 200 $7.95

To Follow His Way: *A Renewal Program for Parishes, Small Groups, Individuals.* By David Knight. SBN 709 $6.95

To order any of these books or cassettes, or for information on all St. Anthony Messenger Press books, tapes and periodicals, write to St. Anthony Messenger Press, 1615 Republic St., Cincinnati, OH 45210, or call 513-241-5615.